AN AUGUSTINE TREASURY

Religious imagery selections
taken from the writings of
SAINT AUGUSTINE

edited by
Jules M. Brady, S.J.
Rockhurst College

ST. PAUL EDITIONS

IMPRIMI POTEST:
   Rev. Leo F. Weber, S.J.

NIHIL OBSTAT:
   Rev. Richard V. Lawlor, S.J.

IMPRIMATUR:
   +Humberto Cardinal Medeiros
   Archbishop of Boston

ACW=Selections from ST. AUGUSTINE, THE FIRST CATECHETICAL INSTRUCTION, ed. by W.J. Burghardt, T. Lawler and J. Quasten, Ancient Christian Writers Series No. 2, and from ST. AUGUSTINE, AGAINST THE ACADEMICS, ed. by W.J. Burghardt, T. Lawler and J. Quasten, ACW No. 12, © 1951 by Johannes Quasten and Joseph C. Plumpe, © 1979 by John J. O'Meara, and from ST. AUGUSTINE, ON THE PSALMS, ed. by W.J. Burghardt, T. Lawler and J. Quasten, ACW Nos. 29 & 30, © 1960, 1961 by Johannes Quasten and Walter J. Burghardt, are reprinted by permission of Paulist Press.

Burnaby=From *Early Christian Fathers*, Volume I, The Library of Christian Classics, newly translated and edited by Cyril C. Richardson. Published in the United States by The Westminster Press, 1953. Used by permission.

FOC=Selections from *Fathers of the Church*, ed., R. J. Deferrari et al., Washington: Catholic University of America Press, 1948-1963. Reprinted by permission.

Library of Congress Cataloging in Publication Data

Augustinus, Aurelius, Saint, Bp. of Hippo.
   An Augustine treasury.

   1. Theology—Collected Works—Early church,
ca. 30-600. I. Brady, Jules M. II. Title.
BR65.A52E6   1980   230'.14   80-16772
ISBN 0-8198-0706-0
ISBN 0-8198-0707-9 (pbk.)

Copyright © 1981, by the Daughters of St. Paul

Printed in U.S.A. by the Daughters of St. Paul
50 St. Paul's Ave., Boston, MA 02130

The Daughters of St. Paul are an international congregation of religious women serving the Church with the communications media.

This anthology is dedicated to my mother
Kathryn Kinsella Brady

Acknowledgements

We hereby thank the publishers who have given their permission to reprint material included in this volume. The Paulist Press has granted us permission to quote from volumes 2, 12, 29 and 30 in the *Ancient Christian Writers* Series. Selections from this series are identified at the end of each quotation by series symbol and volume number. All four Augustine volumes in this series were published by the Newman Press. ACW 2, copyright 1946 by the Editors, was translated by the Rev. Joseph P. Christopher; ACW 12, copyright 1951 by Rev. Johannes Quasten and Rev. Joseph C. Plumpe, was translated by John J. O'Meara; ACW 29 and ACW 30, © copyright by Rev. Johannes Quasten and Rev. Walter J. Burghardt, S.J., in 1960 for ACW 29 and in 1961 for ACW 30, were translated by Dame Scholastica Hebgin and Dame Felicitas Corrigan. The Catholic University of America Press has permitted us to quote passages from volumes, 2, 4, 5, 6, 7, 9, 11, 12, 13, 15, 16, 17 and 18 in the *Fathers of the Church* Series. Selections from this series are identified at the end of each quotation by series symbol and volume number. FOC 2 was published by CIMA Publishing Co. Inc. FOC 18 was published by the Catholic University of America Press. All the other volumes listed above in this series were published by the Fathers of the Church, Inc. Translators of these volumes are as follows: FOC 2, *On Music*, Robert Catesby Taliaferro, *Faith in Things Unseen*, Roy Joseph Deferrari and Mary Francis McDonald, O.P.; FOC 4, *Christian Doctrine*, John J. Gavigan, O.S.A., *The Christian Combat*, Robert P. Russell, O.S.A.; FOC 5, Vernon J. Bourke; FOC 6, Demetrius B. Zema, S.J. and Gerald G. Walsh, S.J.; FOC 7, Gerald G. Walsh, S.J. and Grace Monahan, O.S.U.; FOC 9, FOC 11, FOC 12, FOC 13, Sister Wilfred Parsons, S.N.D.; FOC 15, *The Creed to Catechumens*, Sister Marie Liguori, I.H.M.; FOC 16, *Against Julian the Heretic*, Matthew A. Schumacher, C.S.C., *Patience*, Sister Luanne Meagher, O.S.B., *The Good of Widowhood for Juliana*, Sister M. Clement Eagan, C.C.V.I.; FOC 17, Sister Mary Sarah Muldowney, R.S.M.; FOC 18, Stephen McKenna, C.SS.R. The Westminster Press has given us permission to use quotations from *Augustine: Later Works*. Selections from this book are identified at the end of each quotation by the name of the editor and are used subject to the following credit line.

From AUGUSTINE: LATER WORKS, LCC, Vol. VIII.

Edited by John Burnaby, Published 1955, SCM

Press, Ltd., London. The Westminster Press,

U.S.A., 1955. Used by permission.

All other selections are from *The Nicene and Post-Nicene Fathers*. We also express our gratitude to Vernon J. Bourke who has allowed us to translate the titles of Augustine's works in the same way for the most part as he has done in his book, *The Essential Augustine*. We conclude with a personal note. I am especially grateful to Vernon J. Bourke for introducing me to the thought of St. Augustine.

CONTENTS

(bold numbers designate the number of quotation)

11		Preface
13	I.	Scripture **1**
15	II.	Knowing God in This Life **3**
27	III.	Omnipresence **15**
36	IV.	Providence **23**
39	V.	Trinity **26**
41	VI.	Creation **28**
43	VII.	Evil **31**
68	VIII.	Self **63**
82	IX.	Teaching **79**
86	X.	Death **85**
88	XI.	Heaven **87**
93	XII.	Happiness **94**
94	XIII.	Sin **95**
101	XIV.	Grace **103**
113	XV.	Faith **118**
116	XVI.	Holy Fear **121**
118	XVII.	Love of God **123**
121	XVIII.	Love of Neighbor **126**
135	XIX.	Use of Creatures **138**
140	XX.	Peace **143**
142	XXI.	Wisdom **144**
144	XXII.	Prayer **146**
150	XXIII.	Humility **153**
154	XXIV.	Christ **158**
200	XXV.	True Christian **210**
202	XXVI.	Church **212**
205	XXVII.	Sacraments **215**
208	XXVIII.	Mass **218**

Abbreviations

ACW: *Ancient Christian Writers*, ed. J. Quasten et al., Westminster, Md.: Newman Press, 1946-1961.

Brady: Nine excerpts from the Sermons of St. Augustine were translated by Jules M. Brady, S.J.

Burnaby: *Augustine: Later Works*, ed. J. Burnaby, Philadelphia: The Westminster Press, 1955.

FOC; *Fathers of the Church*, ed. R.J. Deferrari et al., Washington: Catholic University of America Press, 1948-1963.

Nicene: A Select Library of the Nicene and Post-Nicene Fathers, 8 vols., ed. Philip Schaff, New York: The Christian Literature Co., 1887-1892.

PREFACE

How did St. Augustine teach religious truth? He describes his religious education technique of blending the spiritual with the material in the following quotation from his *Letter 55*, to Januarius. *We make use of parables, formulated with reverent devotion, to illustrate our religion, drawing freely in our speech on the whole creation, the winds, the sea, the earth, birds, fishes, flocks, trees, men.* This anthology is a collection of passages written by Augustine in which each selection exemplifies how the Bishop of Hippo follows his own formula for teaching religious truth: tie the truth to a concrete image. Thus the theme of these quotations from the sermons, letters and books of Augustine is appropriately expressed in the sub-title of this volume, *Religious imagery selections*. These texts have been taken from available English translations and are arranged according to topics. Who can fail to be delighted by the beauty of these passages?

This is not a book to be read from cover to cover at one sitting. Rather a reader should study one selection each day, close the book and then reflect prayerfully on the meaning of the text. In this way *An Augustine Treasury* will provide daily spiritual meditation material for more than six months.

I. SCRIPTURE

1.   For if two men, Ishmael and Isaac, are types of the two covenants, can it be supposed that there is no significance in the vast number of particulars which have no historical or natural value? Suppose we were to see some Hebrew characters written on the wall of a noble building, should we be so foolish as to conclude that, because we cannot understand the characters, they are not intended to be read, and are mere painting, without any meaning? So, whoever with a candid mind reads all these things that are contained in the Old Testament Scriptures must feel constrained to acknowledge that they have a meaning.

Against Faustus the Manichee, XII, 37;
trans. Nicene, 4, 195.

2.   As for the books of the apostles and prophets, we read them as a record of our faith, to encourage our hope and animate our love. These books are in perfect harmony with one another; and their harmony, like the music of a heavenly trumpet, wakens us from the torpor of worldliness, and urges us on to the prize of our high calling. The apostle, after quoting from the prophets the words, *The reproaches of them that reproached Thee fell on me*, goes on to speak of the benefit of reading the prophets: *For whatsoever things were* *written beforetime were written for our learning; that we, through patience and comfort of the Scriptures, might have hope.* (Rom. 15:4) If Faustus denies this, we can only say with Paul, *If any one shall preach to you another doctrine than that ye have received, let him be accursed.* (Gal. 1:9)

Against Faustus the Manichee, XIII, 18;
trans. Nicene, 4, 207.

II. KNOWING GOD IN THIS LIFE

3. *No man hath seen God at any time.* God is an invisible reality: he is to be sought, not with the eye, but with the heart. If we would see the light of the sun, we must keep clear the bodily eye which is our means of beholding it. So if we would see God, let us cleanse the eye with which God can be seen. And the place of that eye we may learn from the Gospel: *Blessed are the pure in heart, for they shall see God.* (Matt. 5:8) Only let not the *desire of the eyes* fashion our thought of God. One may easily imagine for oneself some vast form, or some measureless immensity extended through space, as it might be this light which our eyes can see, increased to the limit and flooding the landscape; or one may picture some old man of venerable aspect. But our thoughts are not to go that way. There is true matter for your thought, if you would see God. *God is love.* What outward appearance, what form, what stature, hands or feet, has love? None can say; and yet love has feet, which take us to the Church, love has hands which give to the poor, love has eyes which give intelligence of him who is in need—as the Psalm says: *Blessed is he who bethinks himself of the needy and poor.* (Ps. 41:1) Love has ears, of which the Lord says: *He that hath ears for hearing, let him hear.* (Luke 8:8) All these are not members set each in their own place: he that has charity sees the whole at once with the understanding's grasp.

Epistle of John to the Parthians, VII, 10;
trans. Burnaby, 317.

4.   Friend, you go through toil and labour, for the love of what? Of avarice. That love must bring toil to the lover: there is no toil in the love of God. Avarice will enjoin upon you the endurance of labours, dangers, wear and tear and troubles; and you will obey, but to what purpose? To gain the wherewithall to fill your purse, and to lose your peace of mind. Peace of mind, I dare say, you had more before you were rich than after you began to be wealthy. See what avarice has charged you with: a houseful of goods, and the fear of thieves; gain of money, and loss of sleep. There is what avarice bade you do, and you have done it. And what is God's charge? *Love me! You may love money and go after it, yet maybe not find it. Whoever seeks me, I am with him. You may love place and position: maybe you will never attain to them. No man has ever loved me and failed of my attaining. You would have a patron or a powerful friend, and you must go about to approach him by way of* *some inferior. Love me* (God says to you); *I have not to be approached through any go-between: love itself sets you in my presence.* My brothers, there can be no sweetness greater than such love.

Epistle of John to the Parthians, X, 4;
trans. Burnaby, 342-343.

5. But since you recall me to primordial natures and substances, my faith is that God Almighty—which must especially be attended to and fixed in the mind—that God Almighty has made good things. But the things made by Him cannot be such as is He who made them. For it is unjust and foolish to believe that works are equal to the workman, things made to the maker. Wherefore if it is reverential to believe that God made all good things, than which nevertheless He is by far more excellent and by far more preeminent; the origin and head of evil is sin, as the apostle said: *Covetousness is the root of all evils; which some following after have made shipwreck of the faith, and have pierced themselves through with many sorrows.* (1 Tim. 6:10)

Disputation against Fortunatus, 21;
trans. Nicene, 4, 120.

6. Let it ever be your supreme thought, that you must love God and your neighbor: *God with all thy heart, and with all thy soul, and with all thy mind; and thy neighbor as thyself.* These must always be pondered, meditated, retained, practiced, and fulfilled. The love of God comes first in the order of enjoying; but in the order of doing, the love of our neighbor comes first. For He who commanded thee this love in two precepts did not charge thee to love thy neighbor first, and then God, but first God, afterwards thy neighbor. Thou, however, as thou dost not yet see God, dost earn to see Him by loving thy neighbor; by loving thy neighbor thou purgest thine eye for seeing God, as John evidently says, *If thou lovest not thy brother whom thou seest, how canst thou love God, whom thou dost not see?* (1 Jo. 4:20)

On the Gospel of John, XVII, 8; trans. Nicene, 7, 114.

7. *But ye,* He adds, *shall know Him; for He shall dwell with you, and be in you.* He will be in them, that He may dwell with them; he will not dwell with them to the end that he may be in them: for the being anywhere is prior to the dwelling there. But to prevent us from imagining that His words, *He shall dwell with you,* were spoken in the same sense as that in which a guest usually dwells with a man in a visible way, He explained what *He shall dwell with you* meant, when He added the words, *He shall be in you.* He is seen, therefore, in an invisible way: nor can we have any knowledge of Him unless He be in us. For it is in a similar way that we come to see our conscience within us: for we see the face of another, but we cannot see our own; but it is our own conscience we see, not another's. And yet

conscience is never anywhere but within us: but the Holy Spirit can be also apart from us, since He is given that He may also be in us. But we cannot see and know Him in the only way in which He may be seen and known, unless He be in us.

On the Gospel of John, LXXIV, 5; trans. Nicene, 7, 335.

8. But how can we follow after Him whom we do not see? or how can we see Him, we who are not only men, but also men of weak understanding? For though God is seen not with the eyes but with the mind, where can such a mind be found as shall, while obscured by foolishness, succeed or even attempt to drink in that light? We must therefore have recourse to the instructions of those whom we have reason to think wise. Thus far argument brings us. For in human things reasoning is employed, not as of greater certainty, but as easier from use. But when we come to divine things, this faculty turns away; it cannot behold; it pants, and gasps, and burns with desire; it falls back from the light of truth, and turns again to its wonted obscurity, not from choice, but from exhaustion. What a dreadful catastrophe is this, that the soul should be reduced to greater helplessness when it is seeking rest from its toil! So, when we are hasting to retire into darkness, it will be well that by the appointment of adorable Wisdom we should be met by the friendly shade of authority, and should be attracted by the wonderful character of its contents, and by the utterances of its pages, which, like shadows, typify and attemper the truth.

Moral Behavior of the Catholic Church, 7.11; trans. Nicene, 4, 44.

9. Whatever pleases you in a work of art brings to your mind the artist who wrought it; much more, when you survey the universe, does the consideration of it evoke praise for its Maker. You look on the heavens; they are God's great work. You behold the earth; God made its numbers of seeds, its varieties of plants, its multitude of animals. Go round the heavens again and back to the earth, leave out nothing; on all sides everything cries out to you of its Author; nay, the very forms of created things are as it were the voices with which they praise their Creator. But who can fathom the whole creation? Who shall set forth its praises? Who shall worthily praise heaven and earth, the sea, and all things that are in them? And these indeed are visible things. Who shall worthily praise the angels, thrones, dominations, principalities, and powers? Who shall worthily praise that power which works actively within ourselves, quickening the body, giving movement to the members, bringing the sense into play, embracing so many things in the memory, distinguishing so many things by the intelligence; who can worthily praise it? Now if in considering these creatures of God human language is so at a loss, what is it to do in regard to the Creator? When words fail, can aught but triumphant music remain? *I have gone round and have offered in His tabernacle a sacrifice of jubilation.*

On Psalm 26, Serm. 2, 12;
trans. ACW 29, 272-273.

10. *Arise, O Lord, judge Thou my cause.* (ver. 22) Because I am not able to show my God, as if I were following an empty thing, they revile me. And not only Heathen, or Jew, or heretic; but sometimes even a Catholic brother doth make a grimace when the promises of God are being preached, when a future resurrection is being foretold. (1 Cor. 15:35) And still even he, though already washed with the water of eternal Salvation, bearing the Sacrament of Christ, perchance saith, *and what man hath yet risen again?* And, *I have not heard my father speaking out of the grave, since I buried him!* God hath given to His servants a law for time, to which let them betake themselves: for what man cometh back from beneath? And what shall I do with such men? Shall I show them what they see not? I am not able: for not for the sake of them ought God to become visible...I see not, he saith: what am I to believe? Thy soul is seen then, I suppose? Fool, thy body is seen: thy soul who doth see? Since therefore thy body alone is seen, why art thou not buried? He marvelleth that I have said, if body alone is seen, why art thou not buried? And he answereth (for he knoweth as much as this), Because I am alive.

How know I that thou art alive, of whom I see not the soul? How know I? Thou wilt answer, Because I speak, because I walk, because I work. Fool, by the operations of the body I know thee to be living, by the works of Creation canst thou not know the Creator? And perchance he that saith, when I shall be dead, afterwards I shall be nothing; hath both learned letters, and hath learned this doctrine from Epicurus, who was a sort of doting philosopher, or rather lover of folly not of wisdom, whom even the philosophers themselves have named the hog: who said that the *chief good* was pleasure of the body; this philosopher they have named the hog, wallowing in carnal mire. From him perchance this lettered man hath learned to say, I shall not be, after I have died. Dried be the rivers of Etham! Perish those doctrines of the Gentiles, flourish the plantations of Jerusalem! Let them see what they can, in heart believe what they cannot see! Certainly all those things which throughout the world now are seen, when God was working Salvation in the midst of the earth, when those things were being spoken of, they were not then as yet: and behold at that time they were foretold, now they are shown as fulfilled, and still the fool saith in his heart, *there is no God.* (Ps. 14:1)

On Psalm 74, 22;
trans. Nicene, 8, 349.

11. Faith then, as it has been elsewhere defined, is *the firm support of those who hope, the* *evidence of things which are not seen.* (Heb. 11:1) If they are not seen, how are they evidenced to be? What! Whence are these things which thou seest, but from That which thou seest not? To be sure thou dost see somewhat that thou mayest believe somewhat, and from that thou seest, mayest believe what thou seest not. Be not ungrateful to Him who hath made thee see, whereby thou mayest be able to believe what as yet thou canst not see. God hath given thee eyes in the body, reason in the heart; arouse the reason of the heart, wake up the interior inhabitant of thine interior eyes, let it take to its windows, examine the creature of God. For there is one within who sees by the eyes. For when thy thoughts within thee are on any other subject, and the inhabitant within is turned away, the things which are before thine eyes thou seest not. For to no purpose are the windows open, when he who looks through them is away. It is not then the eyes that see, but some one sees by the eyes; awake him, arouse him. For this hath not been denied thee; God hath made thee a rational animal, set thee over the cattle, formed thee after His Own image. Oughtest thou to use them as the cattle do; only to see what to add to thy belly, not to thy soul? Stir up, I say, the eye of reason, use thine eyes as a man should, consider the heaven and earth, the ornaments of the heaven, the fruitfulness of the earth, the flight of the birds, the swimming of the fish, the virtue of the seeds, the order of the seasons; consider the works, and seek for the Author; take a view of what thou seest, and seek Him whom thou seest not. Believe in Him whom thou seest not, because of these things which thou seest. And lest thou think that it is with mine own words that I have exhorted thee; hear the Apostle saying, *For the invisible things of God from the creation of the world are clearly seen by those things which are made.* (Rom. 1:20)

Sermon 76, 3;
trans. Nicene, 6, 481-482.

12. For since the creation of the world His invisible attributes are clearly seen—His everlasting power also and divinity—being understood through the things that are made. As we listen, the passage (Rom. 1:18-25), now understood, becomes clear. For why would one notice works and not seek the Workman? You direct your attention to the productive soil; you see the water full of its aquatic animals; you note that the air is beaten by winged creatures; you gaze at the heavens studded with stars; finally, you notice other manifestations of power—and do you not seek the Maker of so glorious a creation? But you say to me: *I see these visible works; I do not see the Maker.* But God gave you your bodily eyes to see His works and your mind to see Him. Neither do you see the soul of man. Therefore, as you recognize the existence of the soul, which you do not see, from the movements and management of the body, so from the management of those very souls and from the administration of the whole world recognize the Creator.

Sermon 197;
trans. FOC 17, 50.

13. *And so they are without excuse.* (Rom. 1:21) Why are they inexcusable? *Seeing that, although they knew God, they did not glorify Him or give thanks. (ibid.)* The Apostle wrote that far from having no knowledge of God, they did know Him.

What is the source of their knowledge about God? They knew Him from the creatures He had made. Notice the beautiful earth, the beautiful sea, the beautiful overarching sky. Observe the splendor of the heavens, the pattern of the stars, and the brilliance of the sun lighting up the day. Look at the moon, whose soft light dispels some of the darkness at night. Watch the animals, some swimming in the sea, others moving about on the surface of the earth, still others flying in the air. Think about the invisible spirits and the observable bodies: the spirits that govern and the bodies that are governed. Reflect on all these creatures and they will cry out to you: Look at us and see our beauty. They confess their beauty. Who created this constantly changing beauty, if not He who is unchanging beauty?

Sermon 241;
trans. Brady.

14. For with what understanding does man grasp God, who does not yet grasp his own understanding itself, whereby he desires to grasp Him? And if he already grasps this, let him carefully note that there is nothing in his own nature better than his own reasoning, and see whether he sees in it any outlines of forms, or the beauty of colors, or the greatness of space, or the distance of parts, or the extension of size, or the movements through intervals of place, or any such things. Of course, we find none of these things in that, than which there is nothing better in our nature, that is, in our mind, by which we apprehend wisdom insofar as we are capable. Therefore, that which we do not find in the best part of ourselves, we should not look for in that which is far better than the best part of ourselves. Accordingly, let us think of God, if we are able, and insofar as we are able, in the following way: as good without quality, as great without quantity, as the Creator who lacks nothing, who rules but from no position, and who contains all things without an external form, as being whole everywhere without limitation of space, as eternal without time, as making mutable things without any change in Himself, and as a Being without passion. Whoever so thinks of God, even though he does not yet discover all that can be known about Him, nevertheless, by his pious frame of mind avoids, as far as possible, the danger of thinking anything about Him which He is not.

On the Trinity, V, 1.2;
trans. FOC 18, 176.

III. OMNIPRESENCE

15. *He was in the world, and the world was made by Him.* Think not that He was in the world as the earth is in the world, as the sky is in the world, as the sun is in the world, the moon and the stars, trees, cattle, and men. He was not thus in the world. But in what manner then? As the Artificer governing what He had made. For He did not make it as a carpenter makes a chest. The chest which he makes is outside the carpenter, and so it is put in another place, while being made; and although the workman is nigh, he sits in another place, and is external to that which he fashions. But God, infused into the world, fashions it; being everywhere present He fashions, and withdraweth not Himself elsewhere, nor doth He, as it were, handle from without, the matter which He fashions. By the presence of His majesty He maketh what He maketh; His presence governs what He made. Therefore was He in the world as the Maker of the world; for, *The world was made by Him, and the world knew Him not.*

On the Gospel of John, II, 10;
trans. Nicene, 7, 16-17.

16. *Jesus answered and said to them, Though I bear witness of myself, my witness is true;*

because I know whence I came and whither I go. The light shows both other things and also itself. Thou lightest a lamp, for instance, to look for thy coat, and the burning lamp affords thee light to find thy coat; dost thou light the lamp to see itself when it burns? A burning lamp is indeed capable at the same time of exposing to view other things which the darkness covered, and also of showing itself to thine eyes. So also the Lord Christ distinguished between His faithful ones and His Jewish enemies, as between light and darkness: as between those whom He illuminated with the ray of faith, and those on whose closed eyes He shed His light. So, too, the sun shines on the face of the sighted and of the blind; both alike standing and facing the sun are shone upon in the flesh, but both are not enlightened in the eyesight. The one sees, the other sees not: the sun is present to both, but one is absent from the present sun. So likewise the Wisdom of God, the Word of God, the Lord Jesus Christ, is everywhere present, because the truth is everywhere, wisdom is everywhere. One man in the east understands justice, another man in the west understands justice; is justice which the one understands a different thing from that which the other understands? In body they are far apart, and yet they have the eyes of their minds on one object. The justice which I, placed here, see, if justice it is, is the same which the just man, separated from me in the flesh by ever so many days' journey, also sees, and is united to me in the light of that justice. Therefore the light bears witness to itself; it opens the sound eyes and is its own witness, that it may be known as the light. But how about the unbelievers? Is it not present to them? It is present also to them, but they have not eyes of the heart with which to see it.

On the Gospel of John, XXXV, 4;
trans. Nicene, 7, 205.

17. We have just heard, brethren, these words of the Lord, which He addressed to His disciples: *Let not your heart be troubled, neither let it be afraid. Ye have heard how I said unto you, I go away, and come unto you: if ye loved me, ye would surely rejoice, because I go unto the Father; for the Father is greater than I.* Their hearts might have become filled with trouble and fear, simply because of His going away from them, even though intending to return; lest, possibly, in the very interval of the shepherd's absence, the wolf should make an onset on the flock. But as God, He abandoned not those from whom He departed as man: and Christ Himself is at once both man and God. And so He both went away in respect of His visible humanity, and remained as regards His Godhead: He went away as regards the nature which is subject to local limitations, and remained in respect of that which is ubiquitous. Why, then, should their heart be troubled and afraid, when His quitting their eyesight was of such a kind as to leave unaltered

His presence in their hearts? Although even God, who has no local bounds to His presence, may depart from the hearts of those who turn away from Him, not with their feet, but with their moral character; just as He comes to such as turn to Him, not with their faces, but in faith, and approach Him in the spirit, and not in the flesh.

On the Gospel of John, LXXVIII, 1; trans. Nicene, 7, 340.

18. You must understand the Word of God, by whom all things were made, without thinking that anything of Him passes away or changes from future to past. He remains as He is and He is everywhere totally present. But He comes when He reveals Himself and goes away when He is hidden. However, He is present whether He is revealed or hidden, as light is present to the eyes of one who sees as well as of one who is blind, but it is present to him who sees as something actual, while to the blind it is something missing. So, also, the sound of the voice is present to ears that hear; it is also present to deaf ears: to the former it is actual, from the latter it is hidden. What is more strange than what happens when our voices utter words in obviously rapid sequence? For, when we speak, there is no chance for even a second syllable until the first has stopped sounding, yet, if one hearer is present, he hears all that we say; and if two are present, both hear the same whole sound which each one hears; and if a silent crowd hears it, they do not divide the sounds among them by particles as if it were food, but the whole sound is heard wholly by all and by each. So, then, is it harder to believe that the eternal Word of God should have the same effect on material things as the word of man has on human ears, and that the Word should be wholly present everywhere, as the sound is heard entirely by each one?

Letter 137, to Volusian; trans. FOC 11, 23.

19.   He does not divide Himself among the hearts or bodies of men in order to dwell in them, giving one part of Himself to this one, another to that one, like the sunlight coming through the doors and windows of houses. He is rather to be compared to sound, although it is a corporeal and transitory thing, which a deaf man does not receive at all, a partly deaf one does not receive entirely, and of those who hear and are equally near it, one receives more than another in proportion as his hearing is keener, another less according as he is harder of hearing, yet the sound itself does not vary from more to less, but in the place where all of them are it is equally present to all. How much more perfect than this is God, whose nature is incorporeal and unchangeably living, who cannot be prolonged and divided like sound by intervals of time, who does not need airy space as a place in which to exist, so as to be near to those who are present, but who remains eternally steadfast in Himself, who can be wholly present to all and to each, and although those in whom He dwells possess Him in proportion to the diversity of their own capacity, some more, some less, He builds up all of them by the grace of His goodness as His most beloved temple! (1 Cor. 3:16)

Letter 187, 19 to Dardanus;
trans. FOC 12, 235-236.

20. If the Word of God occurs to you under the idea of the light of this sun, expand, extend it how you will, set no bounds in your thought to that light; it is nothing to the Word of God. Whatsoever of this sort the mind conceives, is less in one part than in the whole. Of the Word conceive as Whole everywhere. Understand ye what I say; because of my stress of time I am limiting myself as much as I can for your sakes. Understand ye what I say. Lo, this light from heaven, which is called by the name of the sun, when it comes forth, it enlightens the earth, unfolds the day, develops forms, distinguishes colours. Great blessing it is, great gift of God to all mortal men; let His works magnify Him. If the sun is so beauteous, what more beauteous than the sun's Maker? And yet look, Brethren; lo, he pours his rays through the whole earth; penetrates open places, the closed resist him; he sends his light through windows, can he also through a wall? To the Word of God all is open, from the Word of God nothing is hid. Observe another difference, how far from the Creator is the creature, especially the bodily creature. When the sun is in the East, it is not in the West. Its light indeed shed from that vast body reaches even to the West; but itself is not there. When it begins to set, then it will be there. When it rises, it is in the East; when it sets, it is in the West. By these operations of his, it has given name to those quarters. Because it is in the East when it rises at the East, it has made it be called the Rising Sun; because it is at the West when it sets at the West, it has made it be called the Setting Sun. At night it is nowhere seen. Is the Word of God so? When It is in the East, is It not in the West; or when It is in the West, is It not in the East? or does It ever leave the earth, and go under or behind the earth? It is Whole everywhere. Who can in words explain this? Who see it? By what means of proof shall I establish to you what I say?

Sermon 70, 2;
trans. Nicene, 6, 468.

21. If anyone goes out from us, and is asked outside what is being done here, he answers, *The Bishop is speaking a word.* I am speaking a word of the Word. But what a word, of what a Word? A mortal word, of the Word Immortal; a changeable word, of the Word Unchangeable; a passing word of the Word Eternal. Nevertheless, consider my word. For I have told you already, the Word of God is Whole everywhere. See, I am speaking a word to you; what I say reaches to all. Now that which I am saying might come to you all, did ye divide what I say? If I were to feed you, to wish to fill not your minds, but your bodies, and to set loaves before you to be satisfied therewith; would ye not divide my loaves among you? Could my loaves come to every one of you? If they came to one only, the rest would have none. But now see, I am speaking, and ye all receive. Nay, not only all receive, but all receive it whole. It comes whole to all, and to each whole. O the marvels of my word! What then is the Word of God? Hear again. I have spoken; what I have spoken, has gone forth to you, and has not gone away from me. It has reached to you, and has not been separated from me. Before I spake, I had it, and ye had not; I spake, and ye began to have, and I lost nothing. O the marvel of my word! What then is the Word of God?

Sermon 70, 3;
trans. Nicene, 6, 468.

22. Why do we marvel at these conflicting powers of the Word of God when the discourse which I utter is apprehended so freely by the senses that the hearer receives it, yet does not confine it? If it were not received, it would give no instruction; if it were confined, it would not reach others. In spite of the fact that this discourse is divided into words and syllables, you do not take individual particles of it as you do of food for your stomach, but you all hear the whole discourse and each individual takes in the whole.

While speaking, I do not fear that one listener may, by hearing me, grasp the whole discourse so that his neighbor can get nothing of it. On the contrary, I wish you to be so attentive that, depriving the ear and mind of no other person, you as individuals may hear the entire discourse and, at the same time, may permit others to hear it, also. Nor is this hearing accomplished at successive periods of time so that, after the discourse which is being delivered has come to you first, it leaves you so that it may go to another person. No, it comes to all at the same time and the whole discourse is apprehended by each individual. And if the entire sermon could be retained in memory, then, just as you all came to hear the whole discourse so you individually would go away bearing the whole discourse with you. How much more readily, then, would the Word of God, through whom all things were made and who, remaining in Himself, renews all things, who is neither confined by places nor restrained by time, neither changed by long or short intervals of time, neither adorned by speech nor terminated by silence, be able to make fertile the womb of His Mother when He assumed human flesh, yet not leave the bosom of His Father; to make His way hither for human eyes to gaze upon Him, and still to enlighten angelic minds; to come down to this earth while ruling the heavens; to become Man here while creating men there?

Sermon 187, 2;
trans. FOC 17, 13-14.

IV. PROVIDENCE

23. Therefore, music, that is, the science or perception of rhythm, is granted by the liberality of God to mortals having rational souls, to teach a great truth. Hence, if a man who is skilled in composing a song knows what lengths to assign to what tones, so that the melody flows and progresses with beauty by a succession of slow and rapid tones, how much more true is it that God permits no periods of time in the birth and death of His creatures—periods which are like the words and syllables in the measure of this temporal life—to proceed either more quickly or more slowly than the recognized and well-defined law of rhythm requires, in this wonderful song of succeeding events, for the wisdom through which He made all things is to be esteemed far above all the arts. When I apply this to the leaves of the tree and the number of our hairs, (Matt. 10:30) how much more is it applicable to the rise and fall of man whose span of life is neither shortened nor prolonged beyond what God, the distributor of time, knows to be in harmony with the control of the universe!

Letter 166, 13 to Jerome;
trans. FOC 12, 18-19.

24. *Thou hast blotted out their name forever to the age of ages.* (ver. 6) The name of the wicked has been blotted out; for they who have come to believe in the true God can no longer be called the wicked. Their name is blotted out *forever:* as long, that is, as this world shall last. *To the age of ages.* Now what is this *age of ages?* Is it not that of which this world is, as it were, an image and shadow? The course of the seasons following one another, the waning and waxing of the moon, the sun returning to the same position year by year, spring, summer, autumn and winter each passing away only to come round again—all this is a kind of imitation of eternity. But the duration underlying an immutable continuity is termed the age of ages. It may be compared with a line of poetry, first conceived in the mind and then uttered by the tongue. The mind gives form to the spoken word; the one fashions an abiding work of art, the other resounds in the air and dies away. Thus, too, the age which passes takes its pattern from that unchangeable age which is termed the age of ages. The latter abides in the divine workmanship, that is to say, in the Wisdom and Power of God, whereas the former is worked out in the government of creation.

On Psalm 9, 7;
trans. ACW 29, 115-116.

25. *For as the height of heaven above the earth, so hath the Lord confirmed His mercy* *toward them that fear Him.* (ver. 11) Observe the heaven: everywhere on every side it covereth the earth, nor is there any part of the earth not covered by the heaven. Men sin beneath heaven: they do all evil deeds beneath the heaven; yet they are covered by the heaven. Thence is light for the eyes, thence air, thence breath, thence rain upon the earth for the sake of its fruits, thence all mercy from heaven. Take away the aid of heaven from the earth: it will fail at once. As then the protection of heaven abideth upon the earth, so doth the Lord's protection abide upon them that fear Him. Thou fearest God, His protection is above thee. But perhaps thou art scourged, and conceivest that God hath forsaken thee. God hath forsaken thee, if the protection of heaven hath forsaken the earth.

On Psalm 103, 15;
trans. Nicene, 8, 508.

V. TRINITY

26. When can a father be found coeval with his son, or a son coeval with his father? that the father may beget, he precedes in age; that the son may be born, he follows in age; but this father coeval with his son, or the son with the father, how can this be? Think of the father as fire and the son as its brilliance; see, we have found coevals. The very instant fire begins, immediately it brings forth brilliance; the fire is not before the brilliance, nor the brilliance after the fire. And if we should ask which begets which, the fire the brilliance or the brilliance the fire, straightway common sense, an inborn wisdom, makes you all cry out: Fire the brilliance, not brilliance the fire. Behold the father beginning, behold the son at the same time, neither coming before nor following after. Behold, therefore, the father beginning; behold the son beginning simultaneously. If I have shown you a father beginning, and a son at the same time beginning, believe in the Father not beginning, and with Him the Son Himself not beginning; the Father eternal, the Son co-eternal.

The Creed to Catechumens, 3, 8;
trans. FOC 15, 296.

27. But the only-begotten Son does not come of God the Father as the whole of creation came from Him, which He created from nothing. He begot the Son of His own substance, He did not make Him out of nothing; He did not beget Him in time, through whom He instituted all time, for, as the flame is not antecedent to the brightness which it produces, so the Father has never been without the Son.

Letter 170, to Maximus;
trans. FOC 12, 63.

VI. CREATION

28. For God has not ordained anything which He did not know beforehand; that which was made was in His Word. The world was made; both was made and was there. How both was made and was there? Because the house which the builder rears was previously in his art; and there, a better house, without age, without decay: however, to show forth his art, he makes a house; and so, in a manner, a house comes forth from a house; and if the house should fall, the art remains. So were all things that are made with the Word of God; because God made all things in wisdom, (Ps. 104:24) and all that He made were known to Him: for He did not learn because He made, but made because He knew. To us they are known, because they are made: to Him, if they had not been known, they would not have been made. Therefore the Word went before. And what was before the Word? Nothing at all.

On the Gospel of John, XXXVII, 8; trans. Nicene, 7, 216.

29. The creature cannot be put on a level with the Creator. Distinguish between Him who made, and that which He made. The bench cannot be put on a level with the mechanic, nor the pillar with its builder; and yet the mechanic, though he made the bench, did not himself create the wood. But the Lord our God, in His omnipotence and by the Word, made what He made. He had no materials out of which to make all that He made, and yet He made it. For they were made because He willed it, they were made because He said it; but. the things made cannot be compared with the Maker. If thou seekest a proper subject of comparison, turn thy mind to the only-begotten Son.

On the Gospel of John, XLII, 10;
trans. Nicene, 7, 237.

30. For whatever God designed to make in the creation already existed in *the Word*; and would not exist in the reality, had it not existed in the Word, just as with you the thing would not exist in the building, had it not existed in your design: even as it is said in the Gospel: *That which was made in Him was life.* (Jo. 1:3-4)

On Psalm 45, 5;
trans. Nicene, 8, 147.

VII. EVIL

31. For, in the same fire, gold gleams and straw smokes; under the same flail the stalk is crushed and the grain threshed; the lees are not mistaken for oil because they have issued from the same press. So, too, the tide of trouble will test, purify, and improve the good, but beat, crush, and wash away the wicked. So it is that, under the weight of the same affliction, the wicked deny and blaspheme God, and the good pray to Him and praise Him. The difference is not in what people suffer but in the way they suffer. The same shaking that makes fetid water stink makes perfume issue a more pleasant odor.

City of God, I, 8;
trans. Foc 6, 29.

32. If no one had sinned, this beautiful world could have been filled with created natures that are good. Even now, with sin in the world, it does not follow that all things are sinful. The great majority of those in heaven preserve the integrity of their nature; and not even the sinfulness of a will refusing to preserve the order of its nature can lessen the beauty of God's total order, designed, as it is, according to the laws of His justice. For, as the beauty of a picture is not dimmed by the dark colors, in their proper place, so the beauty of the universe of creatures, if one has insight to discern it, is not marred by sins, even though sin itself is an ugly blotch.

City of God, XI, 23;
trans. FOC 7, 222.

33. So, again, many who have never desired another man's wife, or procured the death of the husband as David did, will never reach the place which David nevertheless held in the divine favor. There is a vast difference between what is in itself so undesirable that it must be utterly rejected, and the rich and plenteous harvest which may afterwards appear. For farmers are best pleased with the fields from which, after weeding them, it may be, of great thistles, they receive a hundred-fold; not with fields which have never had any thistles and hardly bear thirty-fold.

Against Faustus the Manichee, XXII, 68;
trans. Nicene, 4, 298.

34. It might be shown that, though Moses slew the Egyptian, without being commanded by God, the action was divinely permitted, as, from the prophetic character of Moses, it prefigured something in the future. Now, however, I do not use this argument, but view the action as having no symbolic meaning. In the light, then, of the eternal law, it was wrong for one who had no legal authority to kill the man, even though he was a bad character, besides being the aggressor. But in minds where great virtue is to come, there is often an early crop of vices, in which we may still discern a disposition for some particular virtue, which will come when the mind is duly cultivated. For as farmers, when they see land bringing forth huge crops, though of weeds, pronounce it good for corn; or when they see wild creepers, which have to be rooted out, still consider the land good for useful vines; and when they see a hill covered with wild olives, conclude that with culture it will produce good fruit: so the disposition of mind which led Moses to take the law into his own hands, to prevent the wrong done to his brother, living among strangers, by a wicked citizen of the country from being unrequited, was not unfit for the production of virtue, but from want of culture gave signs of its productiveness in an unjustifiable manner.

Against Faustus the Manichee, XXII, 70; trans. Nicene, 4, 299.

35. If, then, any one reading of the action of David, of which he repented when the Lord rebuked and threatened him, find in the narrative an encouragement to sin, is Scripture to be blamed for this? Is not the man's own guilt in proportion to the abuse which he makes for his own injury or destruction of what was written for his recover and release? David is set forth as a great example of repentance, because men who fall into sin either proudly disregard the cure of repentance, or lose themselves in despair of obtaining salvation or of meriting pardon. The example is for the benefit of the sick, not for the injury of those in health. If madmen destroy themselves, or if evil-doers destroy others, with surgical instruments, it is not the fault of surgery.

Against Faustus the Manichee, XXII, 97;
trans. Nicene, 4, 311.

36. Why, then, dost thou fear? Walk in the Lord thy God; be thou assured, what he does not wish thee to suffer thou dost not suffer; what He permits thee to suffer is the scourge of one correcting, not the punishment of one condemning. We are being educated for an eternal inheritance, and do we spurn to be scourged? My brethren, if a boy were to refuse the punishment of cuffs or stripes from his father, would he not be called proud, incorrigible, ungrateful towards paternal discipline? And for what does an earthly father educate his son? That he may not lose the temporal things which he has acquired for him, which he has collected for him, which he does not wish him to lose, which he who leaves them cannot retain eternally. He does not teach a son with whom he is to possess, but one who is to possess after him. My brethren, if a father teaches a son who is to succeed him, and teaches him also that he will have to pass through all these things, in same way as he who is admonishing him is destined to pass through them, how do you wish that He educate us, our Father to whom we are not to succeed, but to whom we are to approach, and with whom we are to abide eternally in an inheritance which does not decay nor die, and which no storms can desolate? He is Himself both the inheritance and the Father. Shall we possess Him, and ought we not to undergo training?

On the Gospel of John, VII, 7;
trans. Nicene 7, 50.

37.   *We know that to them that love God, all things work together unto good.* (Rom. 8:28) He says *All things;* therefore, not only those that are sought after as pleasant, but also those that are avoided as unpleasant, since we use the former without being ensnared, and we beat off the latter without being bruised, while we follow the divine precept by giving thanks in all to Him of whom we say: *I will bless the Lord at all times, his praise shall be always in my mouth.* (Ps. 33:2) *It is good for me that thou hast humbled me, that I may learn thy justifications.* (Ps. 118:71) Indeed, noble lady, deservedly esteemed and most excellent daughter, the human soul would not sigh for that harbor of true and certain salvation if the calm of a deceitful prosperity were always to smile upon us here.

Letter 131, to Proba;
trans. FOC 11, 4.

38.   But, we often have to act with a sort of kindly harshness, when we are trying to make unwilling souls yield, because we have to consider their welfare rather than their inclination, and this sort of thing has been lavishly praised in their literature describing the beginnings of the state. For, in punishing a son, however harshly, a father's love is certainly not cast aside, yet what he does not want, and what makes him suffer, happens because it appears that he can be cured only by unwilling suffering. Thus, if the earthly state observes those Christian teachings, even war will not be waged without kindness, and it will be easier for a society whose peace is based on piety and justice to take thought for the conquered. He whose freedom to do wrong is taken away suffers a useful form of restraint, since nothing is more unfortunate than the good fortune of sinners, who grow bold by not being punished—a penalty in itself—and whose evil will is strengthened by the enemy within. But the depraved and distorted hearts of men esteem human fortunes happy when the splendor of buildings is in evidence, and the collapse of souls is not noticed; when magnificent theaters are erected, and the foundations of virtue are undermined; when the madness of extravagance is glorified, and the works of mercy are scoffed at; when actors live in luxury at the expense of the excessively wealthy, and the poor scarcely have the necessaries of life; when God, who thunders against this public evil through the public voices of His doctrine, is blasphemed by impious nations, and the kind of gods sought after are those whose worship is attended by that theatrical degradation of the body and soul. If God permits these abuses to flourish, it is a sign of His greater wrath; if He lets them go unpunished, that is a very deadly punishment. But, when He withdraws the sustenance of vice and impoverishes the riches of lust, He opposes them in mercy, for it would be a sign of mercy—if that were possible—that even wars should be waged by the good, in order to curb licentious passions by destroying those vices which should have been rooted out and suppressed by the rightful government.

Letter 138, to Marcellinus;
trans. FOC 11, 46-47.

39. God is good, God is just, God is almighty: only a madman doubts this. Therefore, a just cause must be assigned to these great sufferings which befall little children. Doubtless, when their elders suffer these afflictions, we are wont to say either that their goodness is being tested, as in the case of Job, or that their sins are being punished, as happened to Herod; and from the examples which God has willed to manifest it is granted men to make a conjecture about others which are hard to understand. But these are older people. Tell me what we are to answer about children, if there are no sins to be punished in them by such sufferings, since there obviously is no virtue to be tested at that age.

Letter 166, 16 to Jerome;
trans. FOC 12, 21-22.

40. But when God accomplishes some good by the correction of older persons, scourging them by the death or suffering of the children who are dear to them, why should these things not happen, since, in those who suffer them, they are as if they had never been, once they are past, and those on whose account they have happened will either be better, if they are converted by these temporal trials, and will resolve to lead a better life; or they will have no defense against condemnation at the last judgment, if they have refused to turn their desires away from this life of anguish toward eternal life. Who knows what reward, in the secret of His judgments, God has in store for these little ones, whose sufferings have served to break down the hardness of their elders or to test their faith or to prove their mercy; who knows what these little ones will receive, for, although they have done no good deed, neither have they sinned, yet they have suffered? When Herod sought to kill the Lord Jesus Christ, and the Innocents were put to death, it is not without reason that the Church receives and honors them among the martyrs.

Letter 166, 18 to Jerome;
trans. FOC 12, 23.

41. You ask, Why does corruption take from nature what God has given to it? It takes nothing but where God permits; and He permits in righteous and well-ordered judgment, according to the degrees of non-intelligent and the deserts of the intelligent creatures. The word uttered passes away as an object of sense, and perishes in silence; and yet the coming and going of these passing words make our speech, and the regular intervals of silence give pleasing and appropriate distinction; and so it is with temporal natures which have this lowest form of beauty, that transition gives them being, and the death of what they give birth to gives them individuality. And if our sense and memory could rightly take in the order and proportions of this beauty, it would so please us, that we should not dare to give the name of corruptions to those imperfections which give rise to the distinction. And when distress comes to us through their peculiar beauty, by the loss of beloved temporal things passing away, we both pay the penalty of our sins, and are exhorted to set our affection on eternal things.

Against the so-called Fundamental Letter of Mani, 41, 47; trans. Nicene, 4, 150.

42. And so many of these things seem to us disordered and perturbed, because we have been sewn into their order according to our merits, not knowing what beautiful thing Divine Providence purposes for us. For, if someone should be put as a statue in an angle of the most spacious and beautiful building, he could not perceive the beauty of the building he himself is a part of. Nor can the soldier in the front line of battle get the order of the whole army. And in a poem, if syllables should live and perceive only so long as they sound, the harmony and beauty of the connected work would in no way please them. For they could not see or approve the whole, since it would be fashioned and perfected by the very passing away of these singulars. So God has ordered the man who sins as vicious, but not viciously. For he has been made vicious by will, thus losing the whole he who obeyed God's precept possessed, and has been ordered in part so who did not will to fulfill the law has been fulfilled by the law.

On Music, VI, 11, 30;
trans. FOC 2, 355-356.

43. *For the Lord loveth judgment and will not forsake His saints.* (ver. 28) When the saints suffer hardships, do not suppose that God either does not judge at all or judges amiss. Will He who bids you judge justly Himself judge wrongly? He *loves judgment and will not forsake His saints.* The manner in which He does so is such that the life of the saints is hidden in Him; whereas now, toiling on earth, they resemble trees seen in winter, destitute of fruits and leaves, hereafter, when He appears like the newly risen sun, the vitality which persisted in the root will become visible in their fruits. He *loves judgment,* then, *and will not forsake His saints.*

On Psalm 36, Serm. 3, 9;
trans. ACW 30, 314-315.

44. *Thou hast turned all his bed in his infirmity.* (ver. 4) By the bed is understood anything earthly. Every soul that is infirm in this life seeketh for itself somewhat whereon to rest, because intensity of labor, and of the soul extended toward God, it can hardly endure perpetually, somewhat it seeketh on earth whereon to rest, and in a manner with a kind of pausing to recline, as are those things which innocent ones love...The innocent man resteth in his house, his family, his wife, his children; in his poverty, his little farm, his orchard planted with his own hand, in some building fabricated with his own study; in these rest the innocent. But yet God willing us not to have love but of life eternal, even with these, though innocent delights, mixeth bitterness, that even in these we may suffer tribulation, and so He turneth all our bed in our infirmity. *Thou hast turned all his bed in his infirmity.* Let him not then complain, when in these things which he hath innocently, he suffereth some tribulations. He is taught to love the better, by the bitterness of the worse; lest going a traveller to his country, he choose the inn instead of his own home.

On Psalm 41, 4;
trans. Nicene, 8, 130.

45. *In anger the peoples Thou shalt bring down.* (ver. 8) Thou art angry and dost bring down, dost rage and save, dost terrify and call.

Thou fillest with tribulations all things, in order that being set in tribulations men may fly to Thee, lest by pleasures and a wrong security they be seduced. From Thee anger is seen, but that of a father. A father is angry with a son, the despiser of his injunctions: being angry with him he boxeth him, striketh, pulleth the ear, draggeth with hand, leadeth to school. How many men have entered, how many men have filled the House of the Lord, in the anger of Him brought down, that is, by tribulations terrified and with faith filled? For to this end tribulation stirreth up; in order to empty the vessel which is full of wickedness, so as that it may be filled with grace.

On Psalm 56, 12;
trans. Nicene, 8, 222.

46. There cometh my pain, there will come my rest also; there cometh my tribulation, there will come my cleansing also. For doth gold glitter in the furnace of the refiner? In a necklace it will glitter, in an ornament it will glitter: let it suffer however the furnace, in order that being cleansed from dross it may come into light. This is the furnace, there is chaff, there gold, there fire, into this bloweth the refiner: in the furnace burneth the chaff, and the gold is cleansed; the one into ashes is turned, of dross the other is cleansed. The furnace is the world, the chaff unrighteous men, the gold just men; the fire tribulation, the refiner God: that which therefore the refiner willeth I do; wherever the Maker setteth me I endure it. I am commanded to endure, He knoweth how to cleanse. Though there burn the chaff to set me on fire, and as if to consume me; that into ashes is burned, I of dross am cleansed. Wherefore? Because *to God my soul shall be made subject: for from Himself is my patience.* (ver. 5)

On Psalm 62, 7;
trans. Nicene, 8, 254.

47. *Love ye your enemies, do good to them that hate you, and pray for them that persecute you.* (Matt. 5:44) Behold thou sufferest persecution, and cursest them from whom thou sufferest: how dost thou imitate the Passions of thy Lord that have gone before, hanging on the cross and saying, *Father, forgive them, for they know not what they do.* (Luke 23:34)

On Psalm 70, 3;
trans. Nicene, 8, 312.

48. *In the day of tribulation I have sought out God.* (ver. 2) Who art thou that doest this thing? In the day of thy tribulation take heed what thou seekest out. If a jail be the cause of tribulation, thou seekest to get forth from jail: if fever be the cause of tribulation, thou seekest health: if hunger be the cause of tribulation, thou seekest fulness: if losses be the cause of tribulation, thou seekest gain: if expatriation be the cause of tribulation, thou seekest the home of thy flesh. And why should I name all things, or when could I name all things? Dost thou wish to be one leaping over? In the day of thy tribulation seek out God: not through God some other thing, but out of tribulation God, that to this end God may take away tribulation, that thou mayest without anxiety cleave unto God. *In the day of my tribulation, I have sought out God:* not any other thing, but *God I have sought out.*

On Psalm 77, 3;
trans. Nicene, 8, 361.

49. Thou hast converted us, we know Thee, and wilt Thou still be angry with the prayer of Thy servant? Thou wilt evidently be angry, in fact, as a father correcting, not as a judge condemning. In such manner evidently Thou wilt be angry, because it hath been written, *My son, drawing near unto the service of God, stand thou in righteousness and in fear, and prepare thy soul for temptation.* (Ecclus. 2:1) Think not that now the wrath of God hath passed away, because thou hast been converted. The wrath of God hath passed away from thee, but only so that it condemn not for everlasting. But He scourgeth, He spareth not: because He scourgeth every son whom He receiveth. (Heb. 12:6) If thou refusest to be scourged, why dost thou desire to be received? He scourgeth every son whom He receiveth. He who did not spare even His only Son, scourgeth every one.

On Psalm 80, 4;
trans. Nicene, 8, 387.

50. Nor was it without a meaning that Noah's ark was made of *square beams,* (Gen. 6:14) which were typical of the form of the Church. For what is it to be made square? Listen to the resemblance of the squared stone: like qualities should the Christian have: for in all his trials he never falls: though pushed, and, as it were, turned over, he falls not: and thus too, whichever way a square stone is turned, it stands erect.

On Psalm 87, 3;
trans. Nicene, 8, 421.

51. *I will visit their offences with the rod, and their sin with scourges.* (ver. 32) It is not the mercy of one that calls them only; but also that chastises and scourges them. Let therefore thy Father's hand be upon thee, and if thou art a good son, repel not chastening; for *what son is there, to whom his father giveth not chastening?* (Heb. 12:7) Let Him chasten him, so long as He takes not from him His mercy: let Him beat him when obstinate, as long as He does not disinherit him. If thou hast well understood the promises of thy Father, fear not to be scourged, but to be disinherited: *for whom the Lord loveth He chasteneth: and scourgeth every son whom He receiveth.* (Heb. 12:6) Does the sinful son spurn chastening, when he sees the only Son without sin scourged?

On Psalm 89, 29,
trans. Nicene, 8, 435.

52. Artists show many of their works to the unskillful; and when the unskillful have pronounced them perfect, the artists polish them still further, as they know what is still wanting to them, so that men wonder at things they had imagined already perfect having received so much additional polish. This happeneth in buildings, and in paintings, and in embroidery, and almost in every species of art. At first they judge it to be already in a manner perfect, so that their eyes desire nothing further: but the judgment of the inexperienced eye is one, and that of the rule of art another. Thus also these Saints were living before the eyes of God, as if faultless, as if perfect, as if Angels: but He who punished all their own affections, knew what was wanting in them. But He punished them not in anger, but in mercy: He punished them that He might perfect what He had begun, not to condemn what he had cast away. God therefore punished all their affections. How did he punish Samuel? Where is this punishment? ...What was said unto Moses was a type, not a punishment. What punishment is death to an old man? What punishment was it, not to enter into that land, into which unworthy men entered? But what is said of Aaron? He also died an old man: his sons succeeded him in the priesthood: his son afterwards ruled in the priesthood: how did He punish Aaron also? (Numb. 20:24-28, 33:38) Samuel also died a holy old man, leaving his sons as his successors. (1 Sam. 8:1, 25:1) I seek for the punishment inflicted upon them, and according to men I find it not: but according to what I know the servants of God suffer every day, they were day by day punished. Read ye, and see the punishments, and ye also who are advanced bear the punishments. Every day they suffered from the obstinate people, every day they suffered from the ungodly livers; and were compelled to live among those whose lives they daily censured. This was their punishment.

On Psalm 99, 10;
trans. Nicene, 8, 486-487.

53. Many filled with good have attributed to themselves what they had, and have wished to boast as in their own righteousnesses, and have said to themselves, I am righteous; I am great: and have become self-complacent. Unto these the Apostle speaketh: *What hast thou, that thou didst not receive?* (1 Cor. 4:7) But God, wishing to prove unto man that whatever he hath he hath from Him, so that with good he may gain humility also, sometimes troubleth him; He turneth away His face from him, and he falleth into temptation; and He showeth him that his righteousness, and his walking aright, was only under His government.

On Psalm 104, 40;
trans. Nicene, 8, 518.

54. And whoever forsaketh the source of his being, and turneth away from his Creator; as a river into the sea, he glides into the bitter wickedness of this world. It is therefore good for him that he turn back, and that God whom he had set behind his back, may be before his face as he returneth; and that the sea of this world, which he had set before his face, when he was gliding on towards it, may become behind him; and that he may so forget what is behind him, that he may *reach forward to what is before him;* (Philip. 3:13) which is profitable for him when once converted...

On Psalm 114, 7;
trans. Nicene, 8, 551.

55. They who seem not to be wealthy in money, seem to themselves to be wealthy in righteousness towards God; and when calamity overtakes them, they justify themselves, accuse God, and say, What wrong have I been guilty of, or, what have I done? Thou repliest: Look back, call to mind thy sins, see if thou hast done nothing. He is somewhat touched in conscience, and returneth to himself, and thinketh of his evil deeds; and when he hath thought of his evil deeds, not even then doth he choose to confess that he deserves his sufferings; but saith, Behold, I have clearly done many things; but I see that many have done worse, and suffer no evil. He is righteous against God. He also therefore is wealthy: he hath his breast puffed out with righteousness; since God seemeth to him to do ill, and he seemeth to himself to suffer unjustly. And if thou gavest him a vessel to pilot, he would be shipwrecked with it: yet he wishes to deprive God of the government of this world, and himself to hold the helm of Creation, and to distribute among all men pains and pleasures, punishments and rewards. Miserable soul! yet why do ye wonder? He is wealthy, but wealthy in iniquity, wealthy in malignity; but is more wealthy in iniquity, in proportion as he seemeth to himself to be wealthy in righteousness.

On Psalm 123, 7;
trans. Nicene, 8, 598.

56.   Is it an evil thing to die by shipwreck, and a good thing to die by fever? Whether he die in this way or in that, ask what sort of man he is who dieth; ask whither he will go after death, not how he is to depart from life...Whatever then happeneth here contrary to our wish, thou wilt know that it happeneth not, save by the will of God, by His providence, by His ordering, by His nod, by His laws: and if we understand not why anything is done, let us grant to His providence that it is not done without reason: so shall we not be blasphemers. For when we begin to argue concerning the works of God, *why is this? why is that?* and *He ought not to have done this, He did this ill;* where is the praise of God? Thou has lost thy Halleluia. Regard all things in such wise as to please God and praise the Creator. For if thou wert to happen to enter the workshop of a smith, thou wouldst not dare to find fault with his bellow, his anvils, his hammers. But take an ignorant man, who knows not for what purpose each thing is, and he findeth fault with all. But if he have not the skill of the workman, and have but the reasoning power of a man, what saith he to himself? Not without reason are the bellows placed here: the workman knoweth wherefore, though I know not. In the shop he dareth not to find fault with the smith, yet in the universe he dareth to find fault with God. Therefore just as *fire, hail, snow, ice, wind of storms, which do His word,* so all things in nature, which seem to foolish persons to be made at random, simply *do His word,* because they are not made save by His command.

On Psalm 148, 9;
trans. Nicene, 8, 676.

57. If he who is over thee be a good man, he is thy nourisher; if a bad man, he is thy tempter. Receive the nourishment in the one case with gladness, and in the temptation show thyself approved. Be thou gold. Regard this world as the furnace of the goldsmith; in one narrow place are there things, gold, chaff, fire. To the two former the fire is applied, the chaff is burned, and the gold purified. A man has yielded to threats, and been led away to the idol's temple: Alas! I bewail the chaff; I see the ashes. Another has not yet yielded to threats nor terrors; has been brought before the judge, and stood firm in his confession, and has not bent down to the idol image; what does the flame with him? Does it not purify the gold? Stand fast then, Brethren, in the Lord; greater in power is He who hath called you. Be not afraid of the threats of the ungodly. Bear with your enemies; in them ye have those for whom ye may pray; let them by no means terrify you. This is saving health, draw out in this feast here from this source; here drink that wherewith ye may be satisfied, and not in those other feasts, that only whereby ye may be maddened. Stand fast in the Lord. Ye are silver, ye shall be gold. This similitude is not our own, it is out of Holy Scripture. Ye have read and heard, *As gold in the furnace hath He tried them, and received them as a burnt-offering.* (Wisd. 3:6) See what ye shall be among the treasures of God. Be ye rich as touching God, not as if to make Him rich, but as to become rich from Him. Let Him replenish you; admit nought else into your heart.

Sermon 12, 12;
trans. Nicene, 6, 302.

58. If a person wants to hit you when your back is turned, he doesn't shout, *Watch out!* All you have read in the Bible, my friends, is God's voice exclaiming, *Watch out!* The sufferings and the tribulations we endure in this life are from the hand of God who intends to improve us in order that we may not be condemned at the end of our life. The trials of this life may seem difficult, severe, and even overwhelming, but in comparison with the eternal flames they are not merely trivial—they are nothing at all. Whether we suffer or whether others suffer, these are only admonitions. All afflictions, my friends, sent to us in this life by God are admonitions and proddings to improve us.

Sermon 22;
trans. Brady.

59.   In this world there is not a man who is not a stranger; though all do not desire to return to their own country. Now by this very journey we are exposed to waves and tempests; but we must needs be at least in the ship. For if there be perils in the ship, without the ship there is certain destruction. For whatever strength of arm he may have who swims in the open sea, yet in time he is carried away and sunk, mastered by the greatness of its waves. Need then there is that we be in the ship, that is, that we be carried in the wood, that we may be able to cross this sea. Now this Wood in which our weakness is carried is the Cross of the Lord, by which we are signed, and delivered from the dangerous tempests of this world. We are exposed to the violence of the waves; but He who helpeth us is God.

Sermon 25, 2;
trans. Nicene, 6, 337.

60.   Let us not, because human affairs seem to be in disorder, fancy that there is no governance of human affairs. For all men are ordered in their proper places; but to every man it seems as though they have no order. Do thou only look to what thou wouldest wish to be; for as thou shalt wish to be, the Master knoweth where to place thee. Look at a painter. Before him are placed various colours, and he knows where to set each colour on. Questionless the sinner hath chosen to be the black colour; does not then the Artist know where to place him? How many parts does the painter finish off with the colour of black? how many ornaments does he make of it? With it he makes the hair, the beard, the eye-brows; he makes the face of white only. Look then to that which thou wouldest wish to be; take no care where He may order thee who cannot err, He knoweth where to place thee. For so we see it happen by the common laws of the world. Some man, for instance, has chosen to be a housebreaker: the law of the judge knows that he has acted contrary to the law: the law of the judge knows where to place him; and orders him most properly. He indeed has lived evilly; but not evilly has the law ordered him. From a housebreaker he will be sentenced to the mines; from the labour of such how great works are constructed? That condemned man's punishment is the city's ornament. So then God knoweth where to place thee. Do not think that thou art disturbing the counsel of God, if thou art minded to be disorderly. Doth not He who knew how to create, know how to order thee? Good were it for thee to strive for this, to be set in a good place. What was said of Judas by the Apostle? *He went unto his own place.* (Acts 1:25) By the operation of course of Divine Providence, because by an evil will he chose to be evil, but God did not by ordering evil make it. But because that evil man himself chose to be a sinner, he did what he would, and suffered what he would not. In that he did what he would, his sin is discovered; in that he suffered what he would not, the order of God is praised.

Sermon 75, 5;
trans. Nicene, 6, 478.

61. Misfortunes in this world are not obstacles? Then what are these obstacles? Suppose someone sees himself weighed down by misfortunes. This is not an obstacle, because it is only misfortune that weighs him down. The martyrs also were weighed down by misfortune but never overwhelmed by it. Watch out for obstacles, because misfortune alone is without power. What is the distinction between misfortune and an obstacle? Misfortune weighs you down, while an obstacle overwhelms you. In misfortune you are able to suffer, to overcome, to remain faithful, and to avoid sin. If you do this, no misfortune can overwhelm you. You are no more harmed by misfortune than an olive is in a press because the press does not blot out the olive but merely forces the oil out. And so if you praise God while weighed down by misfortune, how beneficial is the press that forces these praises out. When put in chains, the Apostles were oppressed by misfortune, and in this misfortune they exclaimed the praises of God.

Sermon 81;
trans. Brady.

62. Don't be irritated by people in love with the world, who want to remain in it, and who—whether they want to or not—must leave it. Don't be misled or seduced by them. Misfortune like this is no obstacle. Live rightly and you will be strengthened by these adversities. When misfortune visits you, you can make it what you wish—either an opportunity for improvement or an occasion of condemnation. As misfortune finds you, so will misfortune be. Misfortune is a fire. If it finds you gold, it will purify you. If it finds you chaff, it will burn you to ashes.

Sermon 81;
trans. Brady.

VIII. SELF

63. Associate with the good, whom you see loving your King with you. For you are like to find many such if such you yourself begin to be. For if at the public shows you desire the company and friendship of those who with you loved a charioteer, or a gladiator, or some actor, how much more should you delight in being associated with those who together with you love God, for whom he that loves Him shall never blush with shame, since not only can He not be conquered Himself, but He shall make those that love Him likewise unconquerable.

On Catechizing the Uninstructed, 25, 49; trans. ACW 2, 81.

64. Of all who can enjoy God with us, we love some whom we help, some by whom we are helped, some whose assistance we stand in need of and whose wants we relieve, some on whom we neither bestow any benefit nor expect that they should bestow any upon us. Nevertheless, we ought to desire that they all love God with us, and all the assistance which we either give them or receive from them must be directed toward that one purpose. In the theaters, places of wickedness, if a man has a fondness for some actor and enjoys his acting as a great, or even as the greatest, good, he likes all who share this fondness with him, not on their own account, but because of the one whom they like in common. The more ardent he is in his own affection for that actor, the more he strives in every possible way to have more people like him, and is all the more anxious to show him off to more people. When he sees anyone somewhat unenthusiastic, he stirs him up as much as he can by his praise of the actor. If he chances upon someone who opposes him, he is greatly vexed at his dislike for the object of his affections and strives in every way he can to remove the feeling. How should we act who are united by the love of God, the enjoyment of whom constitutes our happy life, from whom all who love Him receive their existence and their love of Him, of whom we have no fear at all that, once known, He could fail to satisfy anyone? He wishes to be loved, not for any benefit to Himself, but that He may grant to those who love Him an everlasting reward, that is, Himself whom they love. Hence it is that we love even our enemies. We do not fear them, since they are unable to snatch from us that which we love; instead, we feel compassion for them, because the more they hate us the farther they sever themselves from Him whom we love. If they would be reconciled to Him, they would have to love Him as the Supreme Good and us as sharers of such a great blessing.

Christian Doctrine, I, 29;
trans. FOC 4, 48-49.

65. What is the source of this monstrosity? What purpose does it serve? Let thy mercy shine forth and let me ask the question, if perchance the mysteries of men's punishments and the darkest griefs of the sons of Adam can answer me. What is the source of this monstrosity? What purpose does it serve? The mind commands the body and is immediately obeyed; the mind commands itself and is resisted. The mind commands the hand to be moved and its readiness is so great that command can hardly be distinguished from enslavement. Yet, the mind is the mind, while the hand is the body. The mind commands the mind to will; it is not something else, yet it does not do it. What is the source of this monstrosity? What purpose does it serve? It commands, I say, that the will-act be performed, and it would not issue the command unless it willed it, yet its command is not carried out.

Confessions, VIII, 9.21;
trans. FOC 5, 217.

66. What do you desire? I ask you. Can it be seen with the eyes? Can it be touched? Is it some fairness which delights the eyes? Are not the martyrs vehemently beloved; and when we commemorate them do we not burn with love? What is it that we love in them, brethren? Limbs torn by wild beasts? What is more revolting if thou askest the eyes of the flesh? what more fair if thou askest the eyes of the heart? How appears in your eyes a very fair young man who is a thief? How shocked are your eyes! Are the eyes of the flesh shocked? If you interrogate them, nothing is more shapely and better formed than that body; the symmetry of the limbs and the beauty of the color attract the eyes; and yet, when thou hearest that he is a thief, your mind recoils from the man. Thou beholdest on the other hand a bent old man, leaning upon a staff, scarcely moving himself, ploughed all over with wrinkles. Thou hearest that he is just: thou lovest and embracest him. Such are the rewards promised to us, my brethren: love such, sigh after such a kingdom, desire such a country, if you wish to arrive at that with which our Lord came, that is, at grace and truth.

On the Gospel of John, III, 21;
trans. Nicene, 7, 25.

67. What then, beloved, are we going to explain that which we have asked, how the Word seeth, how the Father is seen by the Word, what the seeing of the Word is? I am not so bold, so rash, as to promise to explain this, for myself or for you: however I estimate your measure, still I know my own. Therefore, if you please, not to delay it longer, let us run over the passage, and see how carnal hearts are troubled by the words of the Lord: to this end troubled, that they may not continue in that which they hold. Let this be wrested from them, as some toy is wrested from children, with which they amuse themselves to their hurt, that, as persons of larger growth, they may have more profitable things planted in them, and may be able to make progress, instead of crawling on the earth. Arise, seek, sigh, pant with desire, and knock at what is shut. But if we do not yet desire, not yet earnestly seek, not yet sigh, we shall only be throwing pearls to all indiscriminately, or finding pearls ourselves, regardless of what kind. Wherefore, beloved, I would move a longing desire in your heart. Good character leads to right understanding: the kind of life leads to another kind of life. One kind of life is earthly, another is heavenly: there is a life of beasts, another of men, and another of angels. The life of beasts is excited with earthly pleasures, seeks earthly pleasures alone, and grovels after them with immoderate desire: the life of angels is alone heavenly; the life of men is midway between that of angels and of beasts. If man lives after the flesh, he is on a level with the beasts; if he lives after the Spirit, he joins in the fellowship of angels. When thou livest after the Spirit, examine even in the angelic life whether thou be small or well-grown.

On the Gospel of John, XVIII, 7; trans. Nicene, 7, 119-120.

68. Yet, after all this supposedly subtle and truly prolix disputation, when I ask you briefly and openly why this vital fire plants the root of warfare in man, so that his flesh lusts against his spirit, and it becomes necessary for his spirit to lust against his flesh (Gal. 5:17)—why he who wills to consent with the vital fire receives a mortal wound—I think the black ink in your book must turn red with blushing. Behold the vital fire which not only does not obey at the decision of the soul, which is the true life of the flesh, but for the most part rises up against the soul's decision in disorderly and ugly movements, so that, unless the spirit lusts against it, this vital fire destroys our good life.

Against Julian the Heretic, III, 13.26; trans. FOC 16, 130.

69. God commands nothing for His own advantage, but for the benefit of the one on whom the commandment rests. Therefore, that man is a true master who does not need his slave, but whose slave needs him. Thus, in the part of Scripture which is called the Old Testament, and at that time when those sacrifices were still offered which are not offered now, this was said: *I have said to the Lord, thou art my God for thou hast no need of my goods.* (Ps: 15:2) Similarly, God has no need of those sacrifices, nor does He ever need any, but they are signs of divinely bestowed favors, intended either to endow the mind with virtues or to help in the attaining of eternal salvation. Their observance and performance are exercises of devotion, useful to us, not to God.

Letter 138, to Marcellinus; trans. FOC 11, 39-40.

70. But examine more carefully even now in what sense we are said to be absent, whether it is because we do not see each other in the flesh, or because our minds do not give and receive communications from each other, that is, we do not converse. For I think, although separated in the flesh by long distance, if we could know each other's thoughts we should be more together than if we were in one place, looking at one another but sitting in silence, giving no sign of words of our inner feeling, showing our minds by no movement of our bodies. Hence you understand that each one is more present to himself than one is to another, because each one is better known to himself than to another, not by beholding his own face which he carries around without seeing it, unless there is a mirror at hand, but by beholding his own conscience which he sees even with his eyes closed.

Letter 267, to Fabiola; trans. FOC 13, 285-286.

71. *A helper in tribulations, which find us out too much.* (ver. 1) Tribulations are many, and in every tribulation unto God must we flee; whether it be a tribulation in our estate, or in our body's health, or about the peril of those dearest to us, or any other thing necessary to the sustaining of this life, refuge ought there to be none at all to a Christian man, other than his Saviour, other than his God, to whom when he has fled, he is strong.

For he will not in himself be strong, nor will he to himself be strength, but He will be his strength, who has become his refuge. But, dearly beloved, among all tribulations of the human soul is no greater tribulation than the consciousness of sin. For if there be no wound herein, and that be sound within man which is called conscience, wherever else he may suffer tribulation, thither will he flee, and there find God.... Ye see, dearly beloved, when trees are cut down and proved by the carpenters, sometimes in the surface they seem as though injured and rotted; but the carpenter looks into the inner marrow as it were of the tree, and if within he find the wood sound, he promises that it will last in a building; nor will he be very anxious about the injured surface, when that which is within he declares sound. Furthermore, to man anything inward than conscience is not found; what then profits it, if what is without is sound, and the marrow of conscience has become rotten. These are close and vehement overmuch, and as this Psalm saith, too great tribulations; yet even in these the Lord hath become a helper by forgiving sin.

On Psalm 46,3;
trans. Nicene, 8, 156.

72. What was said by God to the serpent? *She shall mark thy head, and thou shalt mark her heel.* (Gen. 3:15) The devil marketh thy heel, in order that when thou slippest he may overthrow thee. He marketh thy heel, do thou mark his head. What is his head? The beginning of an evil suggestion. When he beginneth to suggest evil thoughts, then do thou thrust him away before pleasure ariseth, and consent followeth; and so shalt thou avoid his head, and he shall not grasp thy heel. But wherefore said He this to Eve? Because through the flesh man doth slip. Our flesh is an Eve within us. *He that loveth his wife,* he saith, *loveth himself.* What meaneth *himself?* He continueth, and saith, *For no man ever yet hath hated his own flesh.* (Eph. 5:28-29) Because then the devil would make us slip through the flesh, just as he made that man Adam to slip, through Eve; Eve is bidden to mark the head of the devil, because the devil marketh her heel.

On Psalm 49, Serm. 1,6;
trans. Nicene, 8, 170.

73. *God, my God, unto Thee from the light I watch.* (ver. 1) What is to watch? It is, not to sleep. What is to sleep? There is a sleep of the soul; there is a sleep of the body. Sleep of body we all ought to have: because if sleep of body is not taken, a man fainteth, the body itself fainteth. For our frail body cannot long sustain a soul watching and on the stretch on active works; if for a long time the soul shall have been intent on active pursuits, the body being frail and earthly holdeth her not, sustaineth her not for ever in activity, and fainteth and falleth. Therefore God hath granted sleep to the body, whereby are recruited the members of the body, in order that they may be able to sustain the soul watching. But of this let us take heed, namely, that our soul herself sleep not: for evil is the sleep of the soul. Good is the sleep of the body, whereby is recruited the health of the body. But the sleep of the soul is to forget her God.

On Psalm 53, 2;
trans. Nicene, 8, 259

74. *Thy holy Temple is marvelous in righteousness.* (ver. 5) These are the good things of that House. He hath not said, Thy holy Temple is marvelous in pillars, marvelous in marbles, marvelous in gilded ceilings; but is *marvelous in righteousness.* Without thou hast eyes wherewith thou mayest see marbles, and gold: within is an eye wherewith may be seen the beauty of righteousness. If there is no beauty in righteousness, why is a righteous old man loved? What bringeth he in body that may please the eyes? Crooked limbs, brow wrinkled, head blanched with gray hairs, dotage everywhere full of plaints. But perchance because thine eyes this decrepit old man pleaseth not, thine ears he pleaseth: with what words? with what song? Even if perchance when a young man he sang well, all with age hath been lost. Doth perchance the sound of his words please thine ears, that can hardly articulate whole words for loss of teeth? Nevertheless, if righteous he is, if another man's goods he coveteth not, if of his own that he possesseth he distributeth to the needy, if he giveth good advice, and soundly judgeth, if he believeth the entire faith, if for his belief in the faith he is ready to expend even those very shattered limbs, for many Martyrs are even old men; why do we love him? What good thing in him do we see with the eyes of the flesh? Not any. There is therefore a kind of beauty in righteousness, which we see with the eye of the heart, and we love, and we kindle with affection: how much men found to love in those same Martyrs, though beasts tear their limbs! Is it possible but that when blood was staining all parts, when with the teeth of monsters their bowels gushed out, the eyes had nothing but objects to shudder at? What was there to be loved, except that in that hideous spectacle of mangled limbs, entire was the beauty of righteousness? These are the good things of the House of God, with these prepare thyself to be satisfied.... *Blessed they which hunger and thirst after righteousness, for they shall be filled.* (Matt. 5:6) *Thy holy Temple is marvelous in righteousness.* And that same temple, brethren, do not imagine to be aught but yourselves. Love ye righteousness, and ye are the Temple of God.

On Psalm 65, 8;
trans. Nicene, 8, 270-271.

75. This I say, brethren, that ye may profit from what ye have heard, and ruminate within yourselves: permit not yourselves to forget, not only by thinking over again upon these subjects, and discoursing upon them, but also by so living. For a good life which is led after God's commands is like a pen, because it is heard writing in our hearts. If it were written on wax, it would easily be blotted out: write it in your hearts, in your character, and it shall never be blotted out.

On Psalm 94, 25;
trans. Nicene, 8, 467.

76. Guard the mouth of thy heart from evil, and thou wilt be innocent: the tongue of thy body will be innocent, thy hands will be innocent; even thy feet will be innocent, thy eyes, thy ears, will be innocent; all thy members will serve under righteousness, because a righteous commander hath thy heart. *Then shall they say among the heathen, the Lord hath done great things for them.* (ver. 2)

On Psalm 126, 5;
trans. Nicene, 8, 604

77. But observe what great difference there is between my actual assertion, and what you suppose me to say. I do not say that the soul is an airy substance; if I did, I should admit that it is a body. For air is a body; as all who understand what they say declare, whenever they speak concerning bodily substances. But you, because I called the soul incorporeal, supposed me not only to predicate mere emptiness of it, but, as the result of such predication, to say that it is "an airy substance;" whereas I must have said both that it has not corporeity, which air has, and that what is filled with air could not be empty. And your own bag similes failed to remind you of this. For when the bags are inflated, what is it but air that is pressed into them? And they are so far from being empty, that by reason of their distension they become even ponderous. But perhaps the breath seems to you to be a different thing from air; although your very breath is nothing else than air in motion; and what this is, can be seen from the shaking of a fan. With respect to any hollow vessels, which you may suppose to be empty, you may ascertain with certainty that they are really full, by lowering them straight into the water, with the mouth downwards. You see no water can get in, by reason of the air with which they are filled. If, however, they are lowered either in the opposite way, with mouth upward, or aslant, they then fill, as the water enters at the same opening where the air passes out and escapes. This could be, of course, more easily proved by performing the experiment, than by a description in writing. This, however, is not the time or place for longer delay on the subject; for whatever may be your perception of the nature of the air, as to whether it has corporeity or not, you certainly ought not to suppose me to have said that the soul is an aerial thing, but absolutely incorporeal.

Soul and Its Origin, IV, 18;
trans. Nicene, 5, 362.

78. The apostle, indeed, purposely selected this general precept, in which he embraced everything, as if this were the voice of the law, prohibiting us from all sin, when he says, *Thou shalt not covet;* for there is no sin committed except by evil concupiscence; so that the law which prohibits this is a good and praiseworthy law. But, when the Holy Ghost withholds His help, which inspires us with a good desire instead of this evil desire (in other words, diffuses love in our hearts), that law, however good in itself, only augments the evil desire by forbidding it. Just as the rush of water which flows incessantly in a particular direction, becomes more violent when it meets with any impediment, and when it has overcome the stoppage, falls in a greater bulk, and with increased impetuosity hurries forward in its downward course. In some strange way the very object which we covet becomes all the more pleasant when it is forbidden. And this is the sin which by the commandment deceives and by it slays, whenever transgression is actually added, which occurs not where there is no law.

On the Spirit and the Letter, 6;
trans. Nicene, 5, 85.

IX. TEACHING

79. And if we pass through streets that are most familiar to us with all the cheerfulness that springs from well-doing, when we happen to be pointing out the way to one who had been in trouble through losing his way, with how much more alacrity and with how much greater joy, in the matter of salutary doctrine, ought we to go over those things which, as far as we are concerned, need not be repeated, when we are escorting through the paths of peace a soul to be pitied, and one wearied with the wanderings of this world, at the bidding of Him who has given that peace to us.

On Catechizing the Uninstructed, 12, 17; trans. ACW 2, 42.

80. Again, if it be distasteful to us to be repeating over and over things that are familiar and suitable for little children, let us suit ourselves to them with a brother's, a father's, and a mother's love, and when once we are linked to them thus in heart these things will seem new even to us. For so great is the power of sympathy, that when people are affected by us as we speak and we by them as they learn, we dwell each in the other and thus both they, as it were, speak in us what they hear, while we, after a fashion, learn in them what we teach. Is it not a common occurrence, that when we are showing to those who have never seen them before certain lovely expanses, whether of town or countryside, which we through often seeing already have been in the habit of passing by without any pleasure, our own delight is renewed by their delight at the novelty of the scene? And the more so, the closer the friendship between them and us; for in proportion as we dwell in them through the bond of love, so do things which were old become new to us also.

On Catechizing the Uninstructed, 12, 17; trans. ACW 2, 41.

81. We do not forecast the outcome of our acts, then, by the sun or the moon, or by yearly or monthly periods, lest we be shipwrecked in the most dangerous storms of human life, cast by our free will onto the rocks of a wretched slavery; but we make use of parables, formulated with reverent devotion, to illustrate our religion, drawing freely in our speech on the whole creation, the winds, the sea, the earth, birds, fishes, flocks, trees, men; just as, in the administration of the sacraments, we use with Christian liberty, but sparingly, water, wheat, wine, oil.

Letter 55, to Januarius; trans. FOC 9, 271.

82. But, all those truths which are presented to us in figures tend, in some manner, to nourish and arouse that flame of love by the impulse of which we are carried upward and inward toward rest, and they stir and enkindle love better than if they were set before us unadorned, without any symbolism of mystery. It is hard to explain the reason for this; nevertheless, it is true that any doctrine suggested under an allegorical form affects and pleases us more, and is more esteemed, than one set forth explicitly in plain words. I believe that the soul makes its response slothfully as long as it is involved in earthly things, but, if it is borne along to corporeal representations and from them to spiritual ones, which are symbolized by those figures, it gains strength by that transition, it is enkindled like fire shaken in a torch, and by that more ardent love it is carried on to rest.

Letter 55, to Januarius;
trans. FOC 9, 277.

83. Whence is this corruption which we find to be the common evil of good things which are not incorruptible? Such an inquirer will soon find the answer if he seeks for truth with great earnestness, and knocks reverently with sustained assiduity. For while man can use words as a kind of sign for the expression of his thoughts, teaching is the work of the incorruptible Truth itself, who is the one true, the one internal Teacher. He became external also, that He might recall us from the external to the internal; and taking on Himself the form of a servant, that He might bring down

His height to the knowledge of those rising up to Him, He condescended to appear in lowliness to the low. In His name let us ask, and through Him let us seek mercy of the Father while making this inquiry. For to answer in a word the question, Whence is corruption? it is hence, because these natures that are capable of corruption were not begotten by God, but made by Him out of nothing; and as we already proved that those natures are good, no one can say with propriety that they were not good as made by God. If it is said that God made them perfectly good, it must be remembered that the only perfect good is God Himself, the maker of those good things.

Against the so-called Fundamental Letter of Mani, 36, 41;
trans. Nicene, 4, 147-148.

84. As, therefore, we speak justly when we say concerning any teacher of literature who is alone in a city, He teaches literature here to everybody,—not that all men learn, but that there is none who learns literature there who does not learn from him,—so we justly say, God teaches all men to come to Christ, not because all come, but because none comes in any other way.

Predestination of the Saints, 14;
trans. Nicene, 5, 505.

X. DEATH

85. By a profound judgment of God it has often been permitted that the good be deprived of the present life by the wicked, lest such suffering be considered itself an evil. What harm is it for beings destined to die to lose the life of the flesh? And what do those who fear death achieve except to die a little later? Whatever misfortune befalls the dying comes from their life, not their death, for, if at death their souls have been such as to be succored by Christian grace, then, indeed, their death is not the sunset of a good life, but the dawn of a better.

Letter 151, to Caecilian;
trans. FOC 11, 274.

86. It is indeed a cause of tears that you do not see your loving brother, a deacon of the Church at Carthage, who revered you greatly for your mode of life and profession of sacred virginity, as you used to see him going in and out, performing his liturgical duties briskly, and that you do not hear from him those admiring words which he poured out with a devoted, respectful, and courteous affection for the sanctity of your sisterly attachment. When these thoughts recur and the force of habit makes its demands, the heart is pierced and tears come forth like heart's blood. But let the heart be lifted up and the eyes will be dry. Yet the loss of those things which you grieve over, which have come to the end of their temporal course, does not mean the destruction of that affection with which Timothy loved and still loves Sapida; it remains and is preserved among his treasures and is hidden with Christ in the Lord. (Col. 3:3) Do those who love gold lose it when they store it away? Do they not feel more secure about it, as far as that may be, when they keep it shut up from their eyes in safer coffers? Does earthly covetousness think it keeps a thing more safely if it does not see what it loves, and does heavenly charity grieve as if it had lost what it has sent before it to the celestial storehouses? Recall that you are called Sapida, and savor *the things that are above where Christ is sitting at the right hand of God*, (Col. 3:2) who deigned to die for us that we, the dead, might live, and that death itself should not be feared by man as if it were destined to consume man, nor should any of the dead for whom Life died be mourned as if he had lost life. These thoughts and others like them are divine consolations for you, which should make human sadness turn away with shame.

Letter 263, to Sapida;
trans. FOC 13, 270-271.

XI. HEAVEN

87. *Blessed are the pure in heart, for they shall see God.* (Matt. 5:8) Brethren, what we are to see is a vision, that neither eye hath seen nor ear hath heard nor hath come up into the heart of man (1 Cor. 2:9) —a vision surpassing all earthly beauties, of gold or silver, of woods or fields, the beauty of sea and sky, of sun, moon, and stars, the beauty of angels: excelling all these things, for all have their beauty from him.

Epistle of John to the Parthians, IV, 5; trans. Burnaby, 289-290.

88. When, therefore, our Lord Jesus Christ shall come, and, as the Apostle Paul also says, will bring to light the hidden things of darkness, and will make manifest the thoughts of the heart, that every man may have praise from God; (1 Cor. 4:5) then, in presence of such a day, lamps will not be needed: no prophet shall then be read to us, no book of an apostle shall be opened; we shall not require the witness of John, we shall not need the Gospel itself. Accordingly all Scriptures shall be taken out of the way, —which, in the night of this world, were as lamps kindled for us that we might not remain in darkness, —when all these are taken away, that they may not shine as if we needed them, and the men of God, by whom these were ministered to us, shall themselves, together with us, behold that true and clear light.

On the Gospel of John, XXXV, 9; trans. Nicene, 7, 207.

89. *Helper in tribulations which have found us too much:* (Ps. 116:4) there is a certain tribulation which we ought to find. Let such tribulations find us: there is a certain tribulation which we ought to seek and to find. What is that? The above-named felicity in this world, abundance of temporal things: that is not indeed tribulation, these are the solaces of our tribulation. Of what tribulation? Of our sojourning. For the very fact that we are not yet with God, the very fact that we are living amid trials and difficulties, that we cannot be without fear, is tribulation: for there is not that peace which is promised us. He that shall not have found this tribulation in his sojourning, doth not think of going home to his father-land. This is tribulation, brethren. Surely now we do good works, when we deal bread to the hungry, home to the stranger, and the like: tribulation even this is. For we find pitiful objects upon whom we show pity; and the pitiful case of pitiful objects maketh us compassionate. How much better now would it be with thee in that place, where thou findest no hungry man whom thou mayest feed, where thou findest no stranger whom thou mayest take in, no naked man whom thou mayest cover, no sick man whom thou mayest visit, no litigant whom thou mayest set at one! For all things in that place are most high, are true, are holy, are everlasting. Our bread in that place is righteousness, our drink there is wisdom, our garment there is immortality, our house is everlasting in the heavens, our steadfastness is immortality: doth sickness cover over? Doth weariness weigh down to sleep? No death, no mitigation: there peace, quiet, joy, righteousness. No enemy hath entrance, no friend falleth away.

On Psalm 50, 22;
trans. Nicene, 8, 186.

90. There all are righteous and holy, who enjoy the word of God without reading, without letters: for what is written to us through pages, they perceive there through the Face of God. What a country! A great country indeed, and wretched are the wanderers from the country.

On Psalm 120, 5;
Trans. Nicene, 8, 590.

91. Behold what Haggai and Zachariah prophesied. Now the *horn of His people* is humble in afflictions, in tribulations, in temptations, in beating of the breast; when will He *exalt the horn of His people?* When the Lord hath come, and our Sun is risen, not the sun which is seen with the eye, and *riseth upon the good and the evil,* (Matt. 5:45) but That whereof is said, To you that hear

God, *the Sun of Righteousness shall rise, and healing in His wings;* (Mal. 4:2) and of whom the proud and wicked shall hereafter say, *The light of righteousness hath not shined unto us, and the sun of righteousness rose not upon us.* (Wisd. 5:6) This shall be our summer. Now during the winter weather the fruits appear not on the stock; thou observest, so to say, dead trees during the winter. He who cannot see truly, thinketh the vine dead; perhaps there is one near it which is really dead; both are alike during winter; the one is alive, the other is dead, but both the life and death are hidden: summer advanceth; then the life of the one shineth brightly, the death of the other is manifested: the splendor of leaves, the abundance of fruit, cometh forth, the vine is clothed in outward appearance from what it hath in its stock. Therefore, brethren, now we are the same as other men: just as they are born, eat, drink, are clothed, pass their life, so also do the saints. Sometimes the very truth deceiveth men, and they say, *Lo, he hath begun to be a Christian: hath he lost his headache?* or, *because he is a Christian, what gaineth he from me?* O dead vine, thou observest near thee a vine that is bare indeed in winter, yet not dead. Summer will come, the Lord will come, our Splendour, that was hidden in the stock, and then *He shall exalt the horn of His people,* after the captivity wherein we live in this mortal life.

On Psalm 148, 10;
trans. Nicene, 8, 676-677.

92. Wherefore, dearly beloved, Catholic plants, Members of Christ, think What a Head ye have! Children of God, think What a Father ye have found. Christians, think What an Inheritance is promised you. Not such as on earth cannot be possessed by children, save when their parents are dead. For no one on earth possesses a father's inheritance, save when he is dead. But we whilst our Father liveth shall possess what He shall give; for that our Father cannot die. I add more, I say more, and say the truth; our Father will Himself be our Inheritance.

Sermon 96, 1;
trans. Nicene, 6, 543.

93. Hence, in heaven we shall not experience need, and, on that account, we shall be happy. For we shall be filled, but it will be with our God; and He will be for us all those things which we here look upon as being of great value. Here you seek for food as for something important; there God will be your food. Here you seek carnal embraces; *but it is good for me to adhere to my God.* (Ps. 72:28) Here you seek for riches; how will you need all things there where you possess Him who made all things? Lastly, to establish you in security by the words of the Apostle, concerning that life he said: *That God may be all in all.* (1 Cor. 15:28)

Sermon 255, 8;
trans. FOC 17, 357.

XII. HAPPINESS

94. The fish is delighted, too, when, failing to notice the hook, it devours the bait. But, when the fisherman begins to draw his line, first the fish's inner parts are dislocated; after that it is dragged to its destruction, away from all the pleasure that its joy in the bait had brought it. So it is with all who imagine they are happy with temporal goods. They have swallowed the hook and wander aimlessly about with it. The time will come for them to experience how much anguish they have devoured in their greediness. The wicked can cause no harm to the good, for they do not deprive them of what they love. No one can take from them the object of their love and the source of their happiness. In fact, bodily suffering makes wicked souls miserable, but, borne with fortitude, it purifies souls that are good.

Christian Combat, 7.8;
trans. FOC 4, 324.

XIII. SIN

95. *Then saith the damsel that kept the door unto Peter, Art thou also one of this man's disciples? He said, I am not.* Lo, the pillar of the greatest strength has at a single breath of air trembled to its foundations. Where is now all that boldness of the promiser, and his overweening confidence in himself beforehand? What now of those words, when he said, *Why cannot I follow Thee now? I will lay down my life for Thy sake.* (Jo. 13:37) Is this the way to follow the Master, to deny his own discipleship? Is it thus that one's life is laid down for the Lord, when one is frightened at a maid-servant's voice, lest it should compel us to the sacrifice? But what wonder, if God foretold what was true, and man presumptuously imagined what was false?

On the Gospel of John, CXIII, 2;
trans. Nicene, 7, 418.

96. If this is our condition in the body of this death (which was certainly not the condition in paradise in the body of that life), then without any doubt it is plain enough whence infants born carnally contract at birth the obligation of sin which is dissolved only when they are reborn spiritually. They do not contract this obligation from human nature as produced by God, but from the wound which the Enemy inflicted on human nature; not an enemy which, as the Manichaeans say, emerged from a nature of evil God did not make, but an enemy angel, once good as the work of God, now evil from his own work. This enemy first wounded and felled himself so that he made others to be, like himself, outcast, and through evil suasion inflicted the wound of prevarication from which the human race limps even in those who walk in the way of God.

Against Julian the Heretic, III, 26.63;
trans. FOC 16, 163.

97. Just as our eyes, not strong enough to look at the sun, nevertheless look gladly upon those things which are illumined by the sun, so souls already able to delight in the beauty of chastity are nevertheless not able forthwith to look at truth itself by which chastity is illumined. Hence, they do not recoil and shudder when it comes to doing something against truth, as they do when some action is proposed against chastity.

On Patience, 20, 40;
trans. FOC 16, 177.

98. *How good is the God of Israel!* But to whom? *To men right in heart.* (ver. 1) To men perverse what? Perverse He seemeth. So also in another Psalm He saith: *With a holy man holy Thou shalt be, and with the innocent man innocent Thou shalt be, and with the perverse man perverse Thou shalt be.* (Ps. 18:25) What is, perverse Thou shalt be with the perverse man? Perverse the perverse man shall think Thee. Not that by any means God is made perverse. Far be it: what He is, He is. But in like manner as the sun appeareth mild to one having clear, sound, healthy, strong eyes, but against weak eyes doth dart hard spears, so to say; the former looking at it doth invigorate, the latter it doth torture, though not being itself changed, but the man being changed: so when thou shalt have begun to be perverse, and to thee God shall seem to be perverse, thou art changed, not He. That therefore to thee will be punishment which to good men is joy. He calling to mind this thing, saith, *How good is the God of Israel to men right in heart!*

On Psalm 73, 6;
trans. Nicene, 8, 335.

99. *And thinkest thou this, O man, that judgest them which do such things, and doest the same, that thou shalt escape the judgment of God? Or despisest thou the riches of His goodness, and forbearance, and long-suffering; not knowing that the long-suffering of God leadeth thee to* *repentance? But thou*, that is, he who answereth and saith, If I displeased God, He would not spare me, hear what he worketh for himself; hear the Apostle; *but after thy hardness and impenitent heart treasurest up into thyself wrath against the day of wrath, and revelation of the righteous judgment of God; who will render to every man according to his deeds.* (Rom. 2:5-6) He therefore increaseth His long-suffering, thou increasest thine iniquity. His treasure will consist in eternal mercy towards those who have not despised His mercy; but thy treasure will be discovered in wrath, and what thou daily layest up by little and little, thou wilt find in the accumulated mass; thou layest up by the grain, but thou wilt find the whole heap. Omit not to watch thy slightest daily sins: rivers are filled from the smallest drops.

On Psalm 94, 5;
trans. Nicene, 8, 461-462.

100. *I walked in the innocence of my heart, in the midst of my house.* (ver. 2) By the middle of his house, he either signifieth the Church herself; for Christ walketh in her: or his own heart; for our inner house is our heart: as he hath explained in the above words, *in the innocence of my heart.* What is the innocence of the heart? The middle of his house? Whoever hath a bad house in this, is driven out of doors. For whoever is oppressed within his heart by a bad conscience, just as any man in consequence of the overflow of a waterspout or of smoke goeth out of his house, suffereth not himself to dwell therein; so he who hath not a quiet heart, cannot happily dwell in his heart. Such men go out of themselves in the bent of their mind, and delight themselves with things without, that affect the body; they seek repose in trifles, in spectacles, in luxuries, in all evils. Wherefore do they wish themselves well without? Because it is not well with them within, so that they may rejoice in a good conscience....

On Psalm 101, 3;
trans. Nicene, 8, 492.

101. And what is it that disorders the eye of the heart? Evil desire, covetousness, injustice, worldly concupiscence, these disorder, close, blind the eye of the heart. And yet when the eye of the body is out of order, how is the physician sought out, what an absence of all delay to open and cleanse it, that that may be healed whereby this outward light is seen! There is running to and fro, no one is still, no one loiters, if even the smallest straw fall into the eye. And God it must be allowed made the sun which we desire to see with sound eyes. Much brighter assuredly is He who made it; nor is the light with which the eye of the mind is concerned of this kind at all. That light is eternal Wisdom. God made thee, O man, after His own image. Would He give thee wherewithal to see the sun which He made, and not give thee wherewithal to see Him who made thee, when He made thee after His own image? He hath given thee this also; both hath He given thee. But much thou dost love these outward eyes, and despisest much that interior eye; it thou dost carry about bruised and wounded. Yea, it would be a punishment to thee, if thy Maker should wish to manifest Himself unto thee; it would be a punishment to thine eye, before that it is cured and healed. For so Adam in paradise sinned, and hid himself from the face of God. As long then as he had the sound heart of a pure conscience, he rejoiced at the presence of God; when that eye was wounded by sin, he began to dread the Divine light, he fled back into the darkness, and the thick covert of the trees, flying from the truth, and anxious for the shade.

Sermon 38, 6;
trans. Nicene, 6, 380-381.

102. With the eye of the mind, therefore, we perceive in that eternal truth, from which all temporal things have been made, the form according to which we are, and by which we effect something either in ourselves or in bodies with a true and right reason. The true knowledge of things, thence conceived, we bear with us as a word, and beget by speaking from within; nor does it depart from us by being born. But in conversing with others we add the service of our voice or of some bodily sign to the word that remains within, in order to produce in the mind of the listener, by a kind of sensible remembrance, something similar to that which does not depart from the mind of the speaker. Thus there is nothing that we do through the members of our body, in our words and actions, by which the conduct of men is approved or disapproved, that is not preceded by the word that has been brought forth within us. For no one willingly does anything which he has not spoken previously in his heart.

On the Trinity, IX, 7.12;
trans. FOC 18, 281-282.

XIV. GRACE

103. But if for some error or sin of our own sadness seizes us, let us not only bear in mind that *an afflicted spirit is a sacrifice to God* (Ps. 50:19) but also the words: *for as water quencheth a flaming fire, so almsgiving quencheth sin;* (Eccli. 3:33) and *for I desire*, He says, *mercy rather than sacrifice.* (Osee 6:6) As, therefore, if we were in danger from fire, we should, of course, run for water with which to extinguish it, and should be thankful if someone showed us water nearby, so if some flame of sin has arisen from the hay of our passions and we are troubled about it, we should be glad when an opportunity for a work of great mercy is given us, as though a wellspring were pointed out to us from which to put out the blaze that had burst forth.

On Catechizing the Uninstructed, 14, 22; trans. ACW 2, 48.

104. The point here is that the first man had been so constituted that if, as a good man, he had relied on the help of God, he could have overcome the bad angel, whereas he was bound to be overcome if he proudly relied on his own will in preference to this wisdom of his maker and helper, God; and he was destined to a merited reward if his will remained firm with the help of God, and to an equally deserved doom if his will wavered because of his desertion from God. Notice here that, whereas the reliance on the help of God was a positive act that was only possible by the help of God, the reliance on his own will was a negative falling away from favors of divine grace, and this was a possibility of his own choice.

There is an analogy to this in living. The act of living in a body is a positive act which is not a matter of choice but is only possible by the help of nourishment; whereas the choice not to live in the body is a negative act which is in our human power, as we see in the case of suicide. Thus, to remain living as one ought to live was not a matter of choice, even in Eden, but depended on the help of God, whereas to live ill, as one ought not to live, was in man's power; therefore, man was justly responsible for the cutting short of his happiness and the incurring of the penalty that followed.

City of God, XIV, 27;
trans. FOC 7, 409.

105. I saw that there was free exercise of will in that man who was first formed. He was so made that absolutely nothing could resist his will, if he had willed to keep the precepts of God. But after he voluntarily sinned, we who have descended from his stock were plunged into necessity. But each one of us can by a little consideration find that what I say is true. For today in our actions before we are implicated by any habit, we have free choice of doing anything or not doing it. But when by that liberty we have done something and the pernicious sweetness and pleasure of that deed has taken hold upon the mind, by its own habit the mind is so implicated that afterwards it cannot conquer what by sinning it has fashioned for itself. We see many who do not wish to swear, but because the tongue has already become habituated, they are not able to prevent those things from going forth from the mouth which we cannot but ascribe to the root of evil. For that I may discuss with you those words, which as they do not withdraw from your mouth so may they be understood by your heart: you swear by the Paraclete. If therefore you wish to find out experimentally whether what I say is true, determine not to swear. You will see, that that habit is borne along as it has become accustomed to be. And this is what wars against the soul, habit formed in the flesh. This is indeed the mind of the flesh, which, as long as it cannot thus be subject to the law of God, so long is it the mind of the flesh; but when the soul has been illuminated it ceases to be the mind of the flesh. For thus it is said the mind of the flesh cannot be subject to the law of God, just as if it were said, that snow cannot be warm. For so long as it is snow, it can in no way be warm. But as the snow is melted by heat, so that it may become warm, so the mind of the flesh, that is, habit formed with the flesh, when our mind has become illuminated, that is, when God has subjected for Himself the whole man to the choice of the divine law, instead of the evil habit of the soul, makes a good habit.

Disputation Against Fortunatus, 22; trans. Nicene, 4, 121.

106. This discern ye then, that the light which enlighteneth is one thing, another that which is enlightened. For also our eyes are called lights; and every man thus swears, touching his eyes, by these lights of his: *So may my lights live.* This is a customary oath. Let these lights, if lights they are, be opened, and shine for thee in thy closed chamber, when the light is not there; they certainly cannot. Therefore, as these which we have in our face, and call lights, when they are both healthy and open, need the help of light from without, —which being removed or not brought in, though they are sound and are open, yet they do not see, —so our mind, which is the eye of the soul, unless it be irradiated by the light of truth, and wondrously shone upon by Him who enlightens and is not enlightened, will not be able to come to wisdom nor to righteousness. For to live righteously is for us the way itself. But how can he on whom the light does not shine but stumble in the way? And hence, in such a way, we have need of seeing, in such a way it is a great thing to see. Now Tobias had the eyes in his face closed, and the son gave his hand to the father; and yet the father, by his instruction, pointed out the way to the son. (Tobit 2:11)

On the Gospel of John, XXXV, 3;
trans. Nicene, 7, 205.

107. I have also written to the priests that if, after the contribution of your Holiness, there is a deficit, they are to make it up from the treasury of the church, provided that you make your offering cheerfully according to each one's inclination, for whether the money is given from yours or that of the church, it is all God's, and your generosity will be much more pleasing than the treasures of the church, as the Apostle says: *Not that I seek the gift, but I seek the fruit.* (Phil. 4:17) Gladden my heart, then, because I wish to rejoice in your fruits, for you are the trees of God, which He deigns through the ministry of such as I am, to water with continual showers.

Letter 268, to the members of Christ;
trans. FOC 13, 288.

108. Now for the commission of sin we get no help from God; but we are not able to do justly, and to fulfil the law of righteousness in every part thereof, except we are helped by God. For as the bodily eye is not helped by the light to turn away therefrom shut or averted, but is helped by it to see, and cannot see at all unless it help it; so God, who is the light of the inner man, helps our mental sight, in order that we may do some good, not according to our own, but according to His righteousness. But if we turn away from him, it is our own act; we then are wise according to the flesh, we then consent to the concupiscence of the flesh for unlawful deeds. When we turn to Him, therefore, God helps us; when we turn away from Him, He forsakes us. But then He helps us even to turn to Him; and this, certainly, is something that light does not do for the eyes of the body.

On the Merits and Remission of Sins and Infant Baptism, II, 5; trans. Nicene, 5, 45-46.

109. What, therefore, is man, using his own will in this life, before he chooses and loves God, except an unjust and impious creature? What is man, I say?—a creature wandering from the Creator unless his Creator is mindful of him and freely chooses and loves him. Of himself he cannot choose or love unless first he be prepared by being chosen and loved, for by choosing blindness he loses his sight, and in his love for laziness he soon grows tired. But, someone may say: How can God take the initiative in choosing and loving the unjust to justify them, since Scripture says: *Thou hatest all the workers of iniquity.* (Ps. 5:7) How, do we think, except in a wonderful and ineffable way? Yet, can we not also see that a good doctor both hates and loves the sick? He hates him because he is sick; he loves him in order to rid him of his illness.

On Patience, 22, 19;
trans. FOC 16, 257.

110. *The sufferings of this time are not worthy to be compared with the glory to come, that shall be revealed in us.* (Rom. 8:18) What is that glory of ours to come, unless it be equality with the angels, and the vision of God? What a gift is bestowed on a blind man by one who restores his eye sight so that he can see the light of day! When cured, the man can find nothing sufficiently worthy to repay his healer; however much he gives, indeed, what gift can equal that which the other has bestowed? Desiring to give as much as he can, he will give him gold, yes, even masses of it; but the other has given him light! If the one would realize that he is repaying absolutely nothing, he should look at his gift in pitch darkness. And as to ourselves? What shall we give to that Physician who heals our inward sight and enables us to behold that very light eternal which is Himself?

On Psalm 36, Serm. 2, 8;
trans. ACW 30, 275.

111. *May God have pity on us, and bless us.* (ver. 1) Let our soul bless the Lord, and let God bless us. When God blesseth us, we grow, and when we bless the Lord, we grow, to us both are profitable. He is not increased by our blessing, nor is He lessened by our cursing. He that curseth the Lord, is himself lessened: he that blesseth the Lord, is himself increased. First, there is in us the blessing of the Lord, and the consequence is that we also bless the Lord. That is the rain, this the fruit. Therefore there is rendered as it were fruit to God the Husbandman, raining upon and tilling us.

On Psalm 67, 1;
trans. Nicene, 8, 281.

112. But Egypt, since it is said to mean affliction, or one who afflicteth, or one who oppresseth, is often used for an emblem of this world; from which we must spiritually withdraw, that we may not be bearing the yoke with unbelievers. (2 Cor. 6:14) For thus each one becometh a fit citizen of the heavenly Jerusalem, when he hath first renounced this world; just as that people could not be led into the land of promise, save first they had departed from Egypt. But as they did not depart thence, until freed by Divine help; so no man is turned away in heart from this world, unless aided by the gift of the Divine mercy.

On Psalm 114, 4;
trans. Nicene, 8, 550.

113. But a Christian ought not to be wealthy, but ought to acknowledge himself poor; and if he hath riches, he ought to know that they are not true riches, so that he may desire others. ...And what is the wealth of our righteousness? How much soever righteousness there may be in us, it is a sort of dew compared to that fountain: compared to that plenteousness it is as a few drops, which may soften our life, and relax our hard iniquity. Let us only desire to be filled with the full fountain of righteousness, let us long to be filled with that abundant richness, of which it is said in the Psalm, *They shall be satisfied with the plenteousness of Thy house: and Thou shalt give them drink out of the torrent of Thy pleasure.* (Ps. 36:8)

On Psalm 123, 8;
trans. Nicene, 8, 598.

114. *Turn our captivity, O Lord, as the torrents in the south.* (ver. 4) Consider, my brethren, what this meaneth...As torrents are turned in the south, so turn our captivity. In a certain passage Scripture saith, in admonishing us concerning good works, *Thy sins also shall melt away, even as the ice in fair warm weather.* (Ecclus. 3:17) Our sins therefore bound us. How? As the cold bindeth the water that it run not. Bound with the frost of our sins, we have frozen. But the south wind is a warm wind: when the south wind blows, the ice melts, and the torrents are filled. Now winter streams are called torrents; for filled with sudden rains they run with great force. We had therefore become frozen in captivity; our sins bound us: the south wind the Holy Spirit hath blown: our sins are forgiven us, we are released from the frost of iniquity; as the ice in fair weather, our sins are melted. Let us run unto our country, as the torrents in the south.

On Psalm 126, 7;
trans. Nicene, 8, 604-605.

115. *Whosoever saith to his brother, Thou fool, shall be in danger of hell fire: But the tongue can no man tame.* Shall all men go into hell fire? God forbid! *Lord, Thou art our refuge from generation to generation:* (Ps. 90:1) Thy wrath is just: Thou sendest no man into hell unjustly. *Whither shall I go from Thy Spirit?* (Ps. 139:7) and whither shall I flee from Thee, but to Thee? Let us then understand, Dearly beloved, that if no man can tame the tongue, we must have recourse to God, that He may tame it. For if thou shouldst wish to tame it, thou canst not, because thou art a man. *The tongue can no man tame.* Observe a like instance to this in the case of those beasts which we do tame. The horse does not tame himself; the camel does not tame himself; the elephant does not tame himself; the viper does not tame himself; the lion does not tame himself; and so also man does not tame himself. But that the horse, and ox, and camel, and elephant, and lion, and viper, may be tamed, man is sought for. Therefore let God be sought too, that man may be tamed.

Sermon 5, 2;
trans. Nicene, 6, 273.

116. *Work out your own salvation with fear and trembling* (Phil. 2:12) and lest hereupon they should attribute ought to themselves, because he said, *Work,* he subjoined immediately, *For it is God who worketh in you both to will and to do of His good pleasure.* (Phil. 2:13) *It is God who worketh in you;* therefore *with fear and trembling,* make a valley, receive the rain. Low grounds are filled, high grounds are dried up. Grace is rain. Why dost thou marvel then, if *God resist the proud, and giveth grace unto the lowly?* (Jas. 4:6) Therefore *with fear and trembling;* that is, with humility. *Be not high-minded, but fear.* (Rom. 11:20) Fear that thou mayest be filled; be not high-minded, lest thou be dried up.

Sermon 81, 3;
trans. Nicene, 6, 502.

117. By what rules, pray, do they judge these things if not by those in which they see how each one ought to live, even though they themselves do not live in the same manner? Where do they see them? For they do not see them in their own nature, since these things are doubtless in the mind, and their minds are admittedly changeable; but it sees these rules as unchangeable, whoever can see even this in them; nor does it see them in any state *(habitus)* of their mind, since these rules are the rules of justice, but their minds are admittedly unjust.

Where are these rules written in which even the unjust man recognizes what is just, and in which he perceives that he ought to have what he does not have? Where, then, are they written except in the book of that light which is called Truth? From thence every just law is transcribed and transferred to the heart of the man who works justice, not by wandering to it, but being as it were impressed upon it, just as the image from the ring passes over into the wax, and yet does not leave the ring. But he who does not work justice, and yet sees what is to be worked, he it is who is turned away from this light, but is still touched by it. But the sin of him who does not even see how he ought to live is indeed more excusable, since he is not a transgressor of a known law; but even such a one is at times touched by the splendor of the truth that is present everywhere when, upon being admonished, he confesses his sin.

On the Trinity, XIV, 15.21;
trans. FOC 18, 440-441.

XV. FAITH

118. *Ye are the light of the world. A city that is set on a hill cannot be hid. Neither do men light a candle, and put it under a bushel, but on a candlestick; that it may give light to all that are in the house: so let your light shine before men, that they may see your good works, and glorify your Father who is in heaven:* (Matt. 5:14-16) but He did not say to them, Ye are come a light into the world, that whosoever believeth on you should not abide in darkness. Such a statement, I maintain, can nowhere be met with. All the saints, therefore, are lights, but they are illuminated by Him through faith; and every one that becomes separated from Him will be enveloped in darkness. But that Light, which enlightens them, cannot become separated from itself; for it is altogether beyond the reach of change. We believe, then, the light that has thus been lit, as the prophet or apostle: but we believe him for this end, that we may not believe on that which is itself enlightened, but, with him, on that Light which has given him light; so that we, too, may be enlightened, not by him, but, along with him, by the same Light as he.

On the Gospel of John, LIV, 4;
trans. Nicene, 7, 297.

119. *The Lord keepeth all their bones, not one of them shall be broken.* (ver. 21) This, however, brethren, we must not take in a material sense. By the bones of the faithful are denoted their foundations. For just as bones are the foundation of our body, so is faith the foundation of the Christian heart. Hence the patience inherent in faith is the fundamental skeleton; its bones cannot be crushed.

On Psalm 33, Serm. 2, 24;
trans. ACW 30, 182.

120. Do not say, *I said it yesterday, I have said it today, I say it every day, I know it perfectly well.* Call thy faith to mind, look into thyself, let thy Creed be as it were a mirror to thee. Therein see thyself, whether thou dost believe all which thou professest to believe, and so rejoice day by day in thy faith. Let it be thy wealth, let it be in a sort the daily clothing of thy soul. Dost thou not always dress thyself when thou risest? So by the daily repetition of thy Creed dress thy soul, lest haply forgetfulness make it bare, and thou remain naked, and that take place which the Apostle saith, (may it be far from thee!) *If so be that being unclothed, we shall not be found naked.* (2 Cor. 5:3) For we shall be clothed by our faith: and this faith is at once a garment and a breastplate; a garment against shame, a breastplate against adversity. But when we shall have arrived at that place where we shall reign, no need will there be to say the Creed. We shall see God; God Himself will be our vision; the vision of God will be the reward of our present faith.

Sermon 8, 13;
trans. Nicene, 6, 288.

XVI. HOLY FEAR

121. What then of the two fears? There is a servile fear, and there is a clean (chaste) fear: there is the fear of suffering punishment, there is another fear of losing righteousness. That fear of suffering punishment is slavish. What great thing is it to fear punishment? The vilest slave and the cruelest robber do so. It is no great thing to fear punishment, but great it is to love righteousness. Has he, then, who loves righteousness no fear? Certainly he has; not of incurring of punishment, but of losing righteousness. My brethren, assure yourselves of it, and draw your inference from that which you love. Some one of you is fond of money. Can I find any one, think you, who is not so? Yet from this very thing which he loves he may understand my meaning. He is afraid of loss: why is he so? Because he loves money. In the same measure that he loves money, is he afraid of losing it. So, then, some one is found to be a lover of righteousness, who at heart is much more afraid of its loss, who dreads more being stripped of his righteousness, than thou of thy money. This is the fear that is clean—this (the fear) that endureth for ever. It is not this that love makes away with, or casteth out, but rather embraces it, and keeps it with it, and possesses it as a companion. For we come to the Lord that we may see Him face to face. And there it is this pure fear that preserves us; for such a fear as that does not disturb, but reassures. The adulterous woman fears the coming of her husband, and the chaste one fears her husband's departure.

On the Gospel of John, XLIII, 7; trans. Nicene, 7, 241.

122. *Therefore,* he saith, *was I made straight unto all Thy commandments.* (ver. 128) I was made straight, doubtless, because I loved them; and I clung by love to them, which were straight, that I might also myself become straight. Then what he addeth, naturally follows: *and every unrighteous way I utterly abhor.* For how could it be that he who loved the straight could do aught save abhor an unrighteous way? For as, if he loved gold and precious stones, he would abhor all that might bring loss of such property: thus, since he loved the commandments of God, he abhorred the path of iniquity, as one of the most savage rocks in the sailor's track, whereon he must needs suffer shipwreck of things so precious. That this may not be his lot, he who saileth on the wood of the Cross with the divine commandments as his freight, steereth far from thence.

On Psalm 119, 127; trans. Nicene, 8, 581-582.

XVII. LOVE OF GOD

123. But, what do I love, when I love Thee? Not the prettiness of a body, not the gracefulness of temporal rhythm, not the brightness of light (that friend of these eyes), not the sweet melodies of songs in every style, not the fragrance of flowers and ointments and spices, not manna and honey, not limbs which can be grasped in fleshly embrace—these I do not love, when I love my God. Yet, I do love something like a light, a voice, an odor, food, an embrace, when I love my God—the light, voice, odor, food, embrace of my inner man, wherein for my soul a light shines, and place does not encompass it, where there is a sound which time does not sweep away, where there is a fragrance which the breeze does not disperse, where there is a flavor which eating does not diminish, and where there is a clinging which satiety does not disentwine. This is what I love, when I love my God.

Confessions, X, 6.8;
trans. FOC 5, 269-270.

124. *Knowledge puffeth up, but charity edifieth.* (1 Cor. 8:1) If you would confess, but not love, you make yourselves like the demons: they confessed the Son of God, they said, *What* *have we to do with thee?* (Matt. 8:29) and they were driven back. Do you confess, and embrace. They feared for their iniquities: do you love the forgiver of your iniquities. But we cannot love God, if we love the world: if we love the world, it will separate us from the love of God which is charity. The apostle makes us ready, then, to have charity dwelling in us. Two loves there are, of the world and of God: if the love of the world dwells in us, the love of God can find no entrance. The love of the world must depart, the love of God come in to dwell: make room for the better love. Once you loved the world, now cease to love it: empty your heart of earthly love and you shall drink of the love divine: charity will begin its dwelling in you, and from charity nothing evil can proceed. Hear then the words of the apostle who now would cleanse you. He sees men's hearts as a field, and in what condition? If he finds weeds, he roots them up; if he finds clean land, he plants—that tree which he would fain plant, which is charity. The weeds that he would root up are love of the world. Hear the rooter-up of weeds: *Love not the world, nor the things that are in the world. If a man love the world, the love of the Father is not in him.*

Epistle of John to the Parthians, II, 8; trans. Burnaby, 273-274.

125. Forasmuch, however, as an inferior righteousness may be said to be competent to this life, whereby the just man lives by faith although absent from the Lord, and, therefore, walking by faith and not yet by sight,—it may be without absurdity said, no doubt, in respect of it, that it is free from sin; for it ought not to be attributed to it as a fault, that it is not as yet sufficient for so great a love to God as is due to the final, complete, and perfect condition thereof. It is one thing to fail at present in attaining to the fulness of love, and another thing to be swayed by no lust. A man ought therefore to abstain from every unlawful desire, although he loves God now far less than it is possible to love Him when He becomes an object of sight; just as in matters connected with the bodily senses, the eye can receive no pleasure from any kind of darkness, although it may be unable to look with a firm sight amidst refulgent light. Only let us see to it that we so constitute the soul of man in this corruptible body, that, although it has not yet swallowed up and consumed the motions of earthly lust in that super-eminent perfection of the love of God, it nevertheless, in that inferior righteousness to which we have referred, gives no consent to the aforesaid lust for the purpose of effecting any unlawful thing.

On the Spirit and the Letter, 65;
trans. Nicene, 5, 112-113.

XVIII. LOVE OF NEIGHBOR

126. Thou hast also given to this good bondswoman of Thine, in whose womb Thou didst create me, O my God, my Mercy, (Ps. 58:18) the great capacity of serving, whenever possible, as a peacemaker between whatever souls were in disagreement and discord. Thus, when she heard from both parties a good many very bitter remarks about each other—the sort of things which bloated and undigested discord usually vomits up when the indigestion of hatred belches forth into sour gossip with a present friend about an absent enemy—she would not reveal anything about one to the other, unless it would be useful in reconciling them.

This would seem but a small good, except that I have had sad experience with countless crowds of people who, through some dreadful and very widespread pestilence of sin, not only run to angry enemies with the statements of their angry enemies, but even add things which were not said. On the contrary, it should be little enough of an obligation for the man who is worthy of his species to refrain from starting or increasing animosities among men by evil talk, if, in fact, one does not even strive to extinguish them by good talk.

Such a person was she, under the influence of Thy teaching as an inner Teacher in the school of her breast.

Confessions, IX, 9.21;
trans. FOC 5, 249.

127. For the Donatists met with the same fate as the accusers of the holy Daniel. (Dan. 6:24) For as the lions were turned against them, so the laws by which they had proposed to crush an innocent victim were turned against the Donatists; save that, through the mercy of Christ, the laws which seemed to be opposed to them are in reality their truest friends; for through their operation many of them have been, and are daily being reformed, and return God thanks that they are reformed, and delivered from their ruinous madness. And those who used to hate are now filled with love; and now that they have recovered their right minds, they congratulate themselves that these most wholesome laws were brought to bear against them, with as much fervency as in their madness they detested them, and are filled with the same spirit of ardent love towards those who yet remain as ourselves, desiring that we should strive in like manner that those with whom they had been like to perish might be saved. For both the physician is irksome to the raging madman, and a father to his undisciplined son, —the former because of the restraint, the latter because of the chastisement which he inflicts; yet both are acting in love. But if they were to neglect their charge, and allow them to perish, this mistaken kindness would more truly be accounted cruelty. For if the horse and mule, which have no understanding, resist with all the force of bites and kicks the efforts of the men who treat their wounds in order to cure them; and yet the men, though they are often exposed to danger from their teeth and heels, and sometimes meet with actual hurt, nevertheless do not desert them till they restore them to health through the pain and annoyance which the healing process gives, —how much more should man refuse to desert his fellow-man, or brother to desert his brother, lest he should perish everlastingly, being himself now able to comprehend the vastness of the boon accorded to himself in his reformation, at the very time that he complained of suffering persecution?

Correction of the Donatists, 2. 7; trans. Nicene, 4, 635.

128. Let your works of mercy, then, proceed from a merciful heart; for then even in your love of enemies you will be showing love of brothers. Do not think that John has given no charge concerning love of one's enemy; for he has said much of brotherly charity, and it is always the brother that you love. How so? you ask. I ask in turn. Why do you love your enemy? Because you wish him to have good health in this life? but suppose that is not in his interest? Because you wish him to be rich? but if riches themselves should rob him of his sight? to marry a wife? but if that should bring him a life of bitterness? To have children? but suppose they turn out badly? Thus there is uncertainty in all the things you seem to desire for your enemy, because you love him: uncertainty everywhere. Let your desire for him be that together with you he may have eternal life: let your desire for him be that he may be your brother. And if that is what you desire in loving your enemy—that he may be your brother—when you love him, you love a brother. You love in him, not what he is, but what you would have him be. Once before, if I remember right, my dear people, I put to you this parable: Imagine the trunk of a tree lying before you: a good carpenter may see such a piece of timber, unhewn, as it was cut in the forest. He loves it at sight, but because he means to make something out of it. The reason for his love is not that it may always remain as it is: as craftsman, he has looked at what it shall be, not as lover at what it is; and his love is set upon what he will make of it, not upon its present state. Even so has God loved us sinners. God, we say, has loved sinners; for we have his word, *They that are whole need not a physician, but they that are sick.* (Matt. 9:12) But surely his love for us sinners is not to the end that we remain in our sin. Like trees from the wood, we have been looked on by the Carpenter, and his thought turns to the building he will make of us, not to the timber that we were. So may you look upon your enemy, standing against you with his angry passion, his biting words, his provoking insults, his unrelenting hate. But in all this you need think only that he is a *man*. You see all the hostility to yourself as of the man's making; and you see in himself God's making. That he was made to be a man, is the act of God: his hatred of you, his malice against you, is his own. And what do you say in your heart? *Lord, have mercy on him: forgive him his sins: put fear in him, and change him.* You love in him, not what he is but what you would have him be; and thus when you love your enemy, you love a brother.

> *Epistle of John to the Parthians,* VIII, 10;
> trans. Burnaby, 323-324.

129. Think not then, my brethren, that when the Lord says, *A new commandment I give unto you, that ye love one another,* there is any overlooking of that greater commandment, which requires us to love the Lord our God with all our heart, and with all our soul, and with all our mind; for along with this seeming oversight, the words *that ye love one another* appear also as if they had no reference to that second commandment, which says, *Thou shalt love thy neighbor as thyself.* For *on these two commandments,* He says, *hang all the law and the prophets.* (Matt. 22:37-40) But both commandments may be found in each of these by those who have good understanding. For, on the one hand, he that loveth God cannot despise His commandment to love his neighbor; and on the other, he who in a holy and spiritual way loveth his neighbor, what doth he love in him but God? That is the love, distinguished from all mundane love, which the Lord specially characterized, when He added, *as I have loved you.* For what was it but God that He loved in us? Not because we had Him, but in order that we might have Him; and that He may lead us on, as I said a little ago, where God is all in all. It is in this way, also, that the physician is properly said to love the sick; and what is it he loves in them but their health, which at all events he desires to recall; not their sickness, which he comes to remove? Let us, then, also so love one another, that, as far as possible, we may by the solicitude of our love be winning one another to have God within us.

On the Gospel of John, LXV, 2; trans. Nicene, 7, 318.

130. If I could give you an account of my days and of the labor I expend at night on other pressing duties, you would be surprised and very sorry at the great burdens which weigh me down, which cannot be put off, and which prevent me from doing those things which you ask and urge me to do, willing though I am and more grieved than I can say at not being able to do them. When I get a little time, free from my obligations to those men who put such pressure upon me that I cannot in any way avoid them, and I ought not to show them contempt, there are plenty of details having a priority on the scraps of time devoted to dictation, and they are such as will not bear delay. There was, for instance, that summary of our conference, a laborious task which fell to me when I saw that no one was willing to lend himself to the reading of such a pile of documents; there was also the letter to the Donatist laity regarding this same conference of ours, which I finished only after several nights of work; there were the two long letters, one to your Charity, the other to the worthy Volusian, which I believe you have now received. At present, I have in hand a book for our friend, Honoratus, in answer to some five questions which he proposed to me, and insisted upon in a letter, and you can see how unsuitable it would be for me not to answer him as soon as possible. Charity, like a nurse caring for her children, gives the weak preference over the strong, not that they are more worthy of love, but more needy of help, and she wishes them to be like the others whom she passes over for a time as a mark of trust, not of contempt. Such necessities cannot be lacking for dictating something, and they prevent me from dictating what I ardently long to do, when a small bit of time is left me between my piled-up duties, which keep me weighed down with other people's ambitions and necessities, and I do not know what else I can do.

Letter 139, to Marcellinus;
trans. FOC 11, 56-57.

131.   *If you then being evil know how to give good gifts to your children, how much more will* *your Father who is in heaven give good things to them that ask Him?* (Matt. 7:11) Is God, then, the Father of evil men? Perish the thought! How, then, does He say *Your Father who is in heaven* to those whom He addresses as *you, being evil,* except that Truth shows both what we are by God's goodness and what we are by human defect, praising the one, correcting the other? Well was it said by Seneca, a contemporary of the Apostles, several of whose letters to the Apostle Paul are extant: *He who hates bad men hates all men.* Yet, bad men are to be loved, so that they may not continue to be bad, just as sick men are to be loved so that they may not remain sick, but may be cured.

Letter 153, to Macedonius;
trans. FOC 11, 291.

132. *Rebuke a wise man and he will love thee?* (Prov. 9:8) Surely, then, we ought not to refrain from reproving and correcting our brother that he may not heedlessly risk death. It happens regularly and it happens often that a man is cast down for a short time while he is being reproved, that he resists and fights back, but afterwards he reflects in solitude where there is no one but God and himself, and where he does not fear the displeasure of men by being corrected, but does fear the displeasure of God by refusing correction; thereafter, he does not repeat the act which was justly censured, but now loves the brother, whom he sees as the enemy of his sin, as much as he hates the sin itself. On the other hand, if he is one of those of whom it is said: *Rebuke the fool and he will go on to hate thee*, (Prov. 9:8) this strife is not born of love, yet it tries and tests the love of the reprover because it does not return hatred for hatred, while the love which prompts him to reprove remains unmoved even when he who is reproved shows his hatred. However, if the one who reproves tries to return evil for evil to the brother who resents his reproof, he was not fit to reprove, but was evidently fit to be reproved himself. Put these rules into practice so that resentment may either not arise among you or, once aroused, may be immediately snuffed out by speedy peace. Try harder to agree among yourselves than to find fault, for, as vinegar corrodes a vessel if it is left in it too long, so anger corrodes the heart if it goes over to the next day.

Letter 210, to Mother Felicitas;
trans. FOC 13, 37-38.

133. One has to bear with patience that which cannot be removed in a hurry. And He Himself furnished and offered an example of this very patience when, before His passion, He bore with the diabolic Judas as a thief before He exposed him as a traitor. And before undergoing bonds and the cross and death, He did not refuse his deceitful lips the kiss of peace.

On Patience, 9, 8;
trans. FOC 16, 243.

134. Let us now attend to the Psalm. *The Lord is the God of vengeance; the God of vengeance hath dealt confidently.* (ver. 1) Dost thou think that He doth not punish? *The God of vengeance* punisheth. What is, *The God of vengeance?* The God of punishments. Thou murmurest surely because the bad are not punished: yet do not murmur, lest thou be among those who are punished. That man hath committed a theft, and liveth: thou murmurest against God, because he who committed a theft on thee dieth not...Therefore, if thou wouldest have another correct his hand, do thou first correct thy tongue: thou wouldest have him correct his heart towards man, correct thy heart towards God; lest perchance, when thou desirest the vengeance of God, if it come, it find thee first. For He will come: He will come, and will judge those who continue in their wickedness, ungrateful for the prolongation of His mercy, for His long-suffering, treasuring up unto themselves wrath against the day of wrath, and revelation of the righteous judgment of God, who will render to every man according to his deeds: (Rom. 2:4-6) because, *The Lord is the God of vengeance,* therefore hath·He *dealt confidently.*

On Psalm 94, 3;
trans. Nicene, 8, 460.

135. I will, therefore, saith he, live separate with a few good men: why should I live in common with crowds? Well: those very few good men, from what crowds have they been strained out? If however these few are all good: it is, nevertheless, a good and praiseworthy design in man, to be with such as have chosen a quiet life; distant from the bustle of the people, from noisy crowds, from the great waves of life, they are as if in harbour. Is there therefore here what joy? that jubilant gladness which is promised? Not as yet; but still groans, still the anxiety of temptations. For even the harbour hath an entrance somewhere or other; if it had not, no ship could enter it; it must therefore be open on some side: but at times on this open side the wind rusheth in; and where there are no rocks, ships dashed together shatter one another. Where then is security, if not even in harbour? And yet it must be confessed, it is true, that persons in harbour are in their degree much better off than when afloat on the main. Let them love one another, as ships in harbour, let them be bound together happily; let them not dash against one another: let absolute equality be preserved there, constancy in love; and when perchance the wind rusheth in from the open side, let there be careful piloting there. Now what will one who perchance presideth over such places, nay, who serveth his brethren, in what are called monasteries, tell me? I will be cautious: I will admit no wicked man. How wilt thou admit no evil one?... Those who are about to enter, do not know themselves; how much less dost thou know them? For many have promised themselves that they were about to fulfil that holy life, which has all things in common, where no man calleth anything his own, who have one soul and one heart in God: (Acts 4:32) they have been put into the furnace, and have cracked. How then knowest thou him who is unknown even to himself?... Where then is security? Here nowhere; in this life nowhere, except solely in the hope of the promise of God. But there, when we shall reach thereunto, is complete security, when the gates are shut, and the bars of the gates of Jerusalem made fast; (Ps. 147:13) there is truly full jubilance, and great delight.

On Psalm 100, 8;
trans. Nicene, 8, 489:

136. But after he had said, *in place of loving me, they detracted from me;* (ver. 3) what doth he add? *But I gave myself unto prayer.* He said not indeed what he prayed, but what can we better understand than for themselves? For they were detracting greatly from Him whom they crucified, when they ridiculed Him as if He were a man, whom in their opinion they had conquered; from which Cross He said, *Father, forgive them, for they know not what they do;* so that while they in the depth of their malignity were rendering evil for good, He in the height of His goodness was rendering good for evil...The divine words then teach us by our Lord's example, that when we feel others ungrateful to us, not only in that they do not repay us with good, but even return evil for good, we should pray; He indeed for others who were raging against Him, or in sorrow, or endangered in faith; but we for ourselves in the first place, that we may by the mercy and aid of God conquer our own mind, by which we are borne on to the desire of revenge, when any detraction is made from us, either in our presence or our absence...

On Psalm 109, 5;
trans. Nicene, 8, 537.

137. When your enemy asks pardon, at once forgive him. And is this much for you to do? Though it were much for thee to love thine enemy when violent against thee, is it much to love a man who is a supplicant before thee? What has thou to say? He was before violent, and then thou hatest him. I had rather thou hadst not hated him even then: I had rather then when thou wert suffering from his violence, thou hadst remembered the Lord, saying, *Father, forgive them, for they know not what they do.* (Luke 23:34) I would have them much wished that even at that time when thine enemy was violent against thee, thou hadst had regard to the Lord thy God speaking thus. But perhaps you will say, He did it, but then He did it as being the Lord, as the Christ, as the Son of God, as the Only-Begotten, as the Word made flesh. But what can I, an infirm and sinful man, do? If thy Lord be too high an example for thee, turn thy thoughts upon thy fellow-servant. The holy Stephen was being stoned, and as they stoned him on bended knees did he pray for his enemies, and say, *Lord, lay not this sin to their charge.* (Acts 7:60) They were casting stones, not asking pardon, yet did he pray for them. I would thou wert like him; reach forth. Why art thou for ever trailing thy heart along the earth? Hear, *Lift up thy heart,* reach forward, love thine enemies. If thou canst not love him in his violence, love him at least when he asks pardon. Love the man who saith to thee, *Brother, I have sinned, forgive me.* If thou then forgive him not, I say not merely, that thou dost blot this prayer out of thine heart, but thou shalt be blotted thyself out of the book of God.

Sermon 6, 16;
trans. Nicene, 6, 279.

XIX. USE OF CREATURES

138. Thus it is that bodily beauty, created as it is by God, is still but a lowly good, fleeting and fleshly, and cannot be loved without sin if it is preferred to God, who from eternity to eternity is Goodness itself. So it is when gold is so loved by a miser that he forgets what he owes to justice. There is nothing wrong with the gold, but there is with the miser. So it is with any created thing. Although it is good, it can be loved both well and ill—well when due order is observed and ill when that order is disturbed.

City of God, XV, 22;
trans. FOC 7, 469.

139. Let us not love the world, nor the things that are in the world. For the things that are in the world are *the desire of the flesh and the desire of the eyes and the pretensions of this life.* The naming of these three forestalls objection. A man might say: *The things that are in the world are what God has made—heaven and earth, sea, sun, moon, stars, and all the furnishings of the heavens. Why should I not love what God has made?* Let God's Spirit indeed be in you to show you that all these things are good; but beware of loving things created and forsaking their Creator.

You find them fair; but how much fairer is he that formed them! Think, my friends: you may learn by a parable, lest Satan get advantage of you, saying as he is wont: *Be happy in God's creation: he made it only for your happiness!* So men's wits are stolen, and they perish in forgetfulness of their Maker: they use the creature with lust instead of temperance, and the Creator is despised. Of such the apostle says: *They worshipped and served the creature rather than the Creator, who is blessed for ever.* (Rom. 1:25) God forbids you not to love them, but he will not have you seek your bliss in them: the end of your esteem for them should be the love of their Maker. Suppose, my brethren, a man should make for his betrothed a ring, and she should prefer the ring given her to the betrothed who made it for her, would not her heart be convicted of infidelity in respect of the very gift of her betrothed, though what she loved were what he gave. Certainly let her love his gift; but if she should say *The ring is enough, I do not want to see his face again*, what should we say of her? Should we not all abhor such frivolity, and charge her with the mind of an adulteress? *Gold is more to you than a husband, a ring more than your betrothed: if it is in you to transfer your love from your betrothed to the ring and not to want the sight of him, he will have given you a pledge not for security but for divorce.* Yet surely the pledge is given by the betrothed, just that in his pledge he himself may be loved. Even so, God has given you all these things: therefore, love him who made them. There is more that he would give you, even himself, their Maker. Though God has made these things, if you love them and are careless of their Creator—if you love the world, must not your love be set down for adulterous?

Epistle of John to the Parthians, II, 11; trans. Burnaby, 275-276.

140. Oh that we were passing our pilgrimage in sighs, and loving not the world, and continually pushing onwards with pious minds to Him who hath called us! Longing is the very bosom of the heart. We shall attain, if with all our power we give way to our longing. Such in our behalf is the object of the divine Scriptures, of the assembling of the people, of the celebration of the sacraments, of holy baptism, of singing God's praise, and of this our own exposition, —that this longing may not only be implanted and germinate, but also expand to such a measure of capacity as to be fit to take in what eye hath not seen, nor ear heard, nor hath entered into the heart of man. But love with me. He who loves God is not much in love with money. And I have but touched on this infirmity, not venturing to say, He loves not money at all, but, He loves not money much; as if money were to be loved, but not in a great degree. Oh, were we loving God worthily, we should have no love at all for money! Money then will be thy means of pilgrimage, not the stimulant of lust; something to use for necessity, not to joy over as a means of delight. Love God, if He has wrought in thee somewhat of that which thou hearest and praisest. Use the world: let not the world hold thee captive. Thou art passing on the journey thou hast begun; thou hast come, again to depart, not to abide. Thou art passing on thy journey, and this life is but a wayside inn. Use money as the traveller at an inn uses table, cup, pitcher, and couch, with the purpose not of remaining, but of leaving them behind. If such you would be, you, who can stir up your hearts and hear me; if such you would be, you will attain to His promises. It is not too much for your strength, for mighty is the hand of Him who hath called you. He hath called you. Call upon Him, say to Him, Thou hast called us, we call upon Thee; see, we have heard Thee calling us, hear us calling upon Thee: lead us whither Thou hast promised; perfect what Thou hast begun; forsake not Thine own gifts; leave not Thine own field; let Thy tender shoots yet be gathered into Thy barn.

On the Gospel of John, XL, 10;
trans. Nicene, 7, 228-229.

141. *Glory and riches shall be in his house.* (ver. 3) For his house is his heart; where, with the praise of God, he liveth in greater riches with the hope of eternal life, than with men flattering, in palaces of marble, with splendidly adorned ceilings, with the fear of everlasting death. *For his righteousness endureth for ever:* this is his glory, there are his riches. While the other's purple, and fine linen, and grand banquets, even when present, are passing away; and when they have come to an end, the burning tongue shall cry out, longing for a drop of water from the finger's end. (Luke 16:24)

On Psalm 112, 3;
trans. Nicene, 8, 547.

142. The accomplishment of righteousness, in that we live here in labour, in toil, in selfrestraint, in fastings, in watchings, in tribulations; this is the exercise of righteousness, to bear this present time, and to fast as it were from this world; not from the food of the body, which we do but seldom; but from the love of the world, which we ought to do always. He then fulfills the law who abstains from this world. For he cannot love that which is eternal, unless he shall cease to love that which is temporal. Consider a man's love: think of it as, so to say, the hand of the soul. If it is holding anything, it cannot hold anything else. But that it may be able to hold what is given to it, it must leave go what it holds already. This I say, see how expressly I say it; *Whoso loveth the world cannot love God; he hath his hand engaged.* God saith to him, *Hold what I give.* He will not leave go what he was holding; he cannot receive what is offered.

Sermon 75, 7;
trans. Nicene, 6, 479.

XX. PEACE

143. But why is it that, when He said, *Peace I leave with you,* He did not add, *my;* but when He said, *I give unto you,* He there made use of it? Is *my* to be understood even where it is not expressed, on the ground that what is expressed once may have a reference to both? Or may it not be that here also we have some underlying truth that has to be asked and sought for, and opened up to those who knock thereat? For what, if by His own peace He meant such to be understood as that which He possesses Himself? whereas the peace, which He leaves us in this world, may more properly be termed our peace than His. For He, who is altogether without sin, has no elements of discord in Himself; while the peace we possess, meanwhile, is such that in the midst of it we have still to be saying, *Forgive us our debts.* (Matt. 6:12) A certain kind of peace, accordingly, we do possess, inasmuch as we delight in the law of God after the inward man: but it is not a full peace, for we see another law in our members warring against the law of our mind. (Rom. 7:22-23) In the same way we have peace in our relations with one another, just because, in mutually loving, we have a mutual confidence in one another: but no more is such a peace as that complete, for we see not the thoughts of one another's hearts; and we have severally better or worse opinions in certain respects of one another than is warranted by the reality. And so that peace, although left us by Him, is our peace: for were it not from Him, we should not be possessing it, such as it is; but such is not the peace He has Himself. And if we keep what we received to the end, then such as He has shall we have, when we shall have no elements of discord of our own, and we shall have no secrets hid from one another in our hearts.

On the Gospel of John, LXXVII, 4;
trans. Nicene, 7, 339-340.

XXI. WISDOM

144. But whether because of the many different troubles of this life, which for your own part, Romanianus, you have experienced; or because of a certain stupor or lethargy or sluggishness of our dull minds; or because we despair of finding, since the star of wisdom does not appear as easily to our minds as does the light to our eyes; or, again, because—and this is the common mistake—men, wrongly thinking that they have already found truth, do not seek with diligence, if they do seek, and even acquire an aversion for such search; it comes about that knowledge is possessed seldom and by the few. And so it happens that the weapons of the Academics, when one joins issue with them, seem to be invincible and, as it were, made by Vulcan—and this not to men of little account, but to men of capacity and long training. Accordingly, while one should employ the oars of all available virtues in rowing against those waves and buffetings of fortune, one should especially implore with all devotion and piety the divine help so that the constant application of oneself to noble pursuits of the mind may hold its course, nor be put astray by any chance from reaching the safe and pleasant harbour of philosophy.

Against the Academics, II, 1;
trans. ACW 12, 65-66.

145. This comparison in which folly is represented as water and wisdom as air, so that the soul coming up from the choking depths of folly into wisdom is suddenly able to breathe, does not seem to me compatible with the authority of our Scriptures; that other comparison is better, where vice or folly is likened to darkness, virtue or wisdom to light, in so far, of course, as resemblance drawn from corporeal sources can be applied to intellectual concepts. Wisdom does not come suddenly, in the manner of one rising from water into air who is able to breathe as much as he needs as soon as he has reached the top of the waves; it comes, rather, by degrees, in the manner of one advancing from darkness into light and being gradually illumined as he progresses. Until this is fully accomplished we say that he is like someone emerging from a very dark cave into the proximity of light, who is illumined more and more as he approaches the exit, and that the light he has comes from the brightness toward which he is advancing, but the darkness still about him is from the blackness out of which he is coming.

Letter 167, 13 to Jerome;
trans. FOC 12, 42-43.

XXII. PRAYER

146.   So we should understand that though God gives not what we wish, he gives what is for our good. When you are ill, you may ask for something that is bad for you, which the physician knows to be so. Suppose you ask for cold water: if it is good for you, the doctor will give it at once; if it is not, he will refuse it, but that does not mean that he does not hearken. In denying you your wish, he has hearkened to you for your health. So let charity, brethren, be in you: let charity be in you, and you need have no care. Even when your request is not granted, you are heard, though you know it not.

Epistle of John to the Parthians, VI, 8; trans. Burnaby, 306.

147.   There is also the almost daily penance of the good and humble among the faithful by which we strike our breasts saying: *Forgive us our debts as we also forgive our debtors.* (Matt. 6:12) For we do not wish to be forgiven for what we doubt not was forgiven in baptism, but certainly we do wish it for those slight but frequent offenses which steal in on our human weakness, and which, if they were added together, would weigh us down and crush us as one great sin would do.

What difference does it make to the shipwrecked whether the ship is swallowed up and sunk by one great wave, or whether the water, seeping by degrees into the hold and being disregarded and overlooked through carelessness, fills the ship and carries it down? This is our reason for being on guard by fasting, almsgiving, and prayers. When we pray: *Forgive us as we forgive,* we show that we have sins to be forgiven, and when we humble our souls by these words we do not cease to do what may be called daily penance.

Letter 265, to Seleuciana;
trans. FOC 13, 281.

148. *But my soul shall rejoice in the Lord,* (ver. 9) as in Him from whom the soul has heard the words: *I am thy salvation:* as one who is not seeking other external wealth, not seeking to surround herself with pleasures and worldly goods, but cleaving to her true Beloved without thought of reward, not looking for delights at His hands, but setting Him up as the sole source of her delight. What, indeed, can be given to me that is better than God? God loves me; God loves each of you. See, He has made the offer, ask what you will. (Matt. 7:7) If the emperor were to say to you: *Ask what you will,* what requests for tribuneships and chief offices of state would pour from your lips! How much you would plan to get for yourself and bestow upon others! God tells you: *Ask what you will.* What are you going to ask? Rack your brains, stir up your greed, stretch and expand your cupidity to the utmost; it is not a mere mortal, but God Almighty who has bidden you: *Ask what you will.* If you are a lover of property, you will want to possess the whole earth, so that every single person born into it shall be your tenant or your slave. And when you own the whole earth, what then? You will ask for the sea, in which, after all, you cannot live. In that piece of acquisitiveness the fishes will come off better than you. But perhaps you will own the islands? Go beyond that too, ask for the air as well, even though you cannot fly in it; extend your covetousness as far as the heavens, call the sun, moon and stars your own, since He who made them all has said: *Ask what you will:* and yet you will find nothing more precious, nothing more excellent than Himself who made them all. Ask for Him who made them, and in Him and from Him you will possess all He had made. All things are precious, for all are beautiful: but what more beautiful than He? They are strong: but what more strong than He? And there is nothing He more desires to give than Himself. If you can find anything better, ask for it. If you ask for anything else, you wrong Him and harm yourself, by preferring what He made before Him, whereas He, its Maker, desires to give you Himself.

On Psalm 34, Serm. 1, 12;
trans. ACW 30, 201-202.

149. In the *house of God* there is a never-ending festival: for there it is not an occasion celebrated once, and then to pass away. The angelic choir makes an eternal *holiday:* the presence of God's face, joy that never fails. This is a *holiday* of such a kind, as neither to be opened by any dawn, nor terminated by any evening. From that everlasting perpetual festivity, a certain sweet and melodious strain strikes on the ears of the heart, provided only the world do not drown the sounds. As he walks in this tabernacle, and contemplates God's wonderful works for the redemption of the faithful, the sound of that festivity charms his ears, and bears the *hart* away to the *waterbrooks.*

But seeing, brethren, so long as *we are at home in this body, we are absent from the Lord;* (2 Cor. 5:6) and *the corruptible body presseth down the soul, and the earthly tabernacle weigheth down the mind that museth on many things;* (Wisd. 9:15) even though we have some way or other dispersed the clouds, by walking as *longing* leads us on, and for a brief while have come within reach of that sound, so that by an effort we may catch something from that *house of God,* yet through the burden, so to speak, of our infirmity, we sink back to our usual level, and relapse to our ordinary state.

On Psalm 42, 8, 9;
trans. Nicene, 8, 134.

150. But guided nations are walking in the Truth, are exulting in Him, are doing good works; and if perchance there cometh in any water (for on sea they are sailing) through the very small holes, through the crevices into the hold, pumping it out by good works, lest by more and more coming it accumulate, and sink the ship, pumping it out daily, fasting, praying, doing almsdeeds, saying with pure heart, *Forgive us our debts, as also we forgive our debtors* (Matt. 6:12)—saying such words walk thou secure, and exult in the way, sing in the way.

On Psalm 67, 7;
trans. Nicene, 8, 284.

151. They who are baptized, and forthwith depart out of this life, come up from the font without any debt; without any debt they leave the world. But they who are baptized and are still kept in this life, contract defilements by reason of their mortal frailty, by which though the ship be not sunk, yet have they need of recourse to the pump. For otherwise by little and little will that enter in by which the whole ship will be sunk. And to offer this prayer, is to have recourse to the pump. But we ought not only to pray, but to do alms also, because when the pump is used to prevent the ship from sinking, both the voices and hands are at work. Now we are at work with our voices, when we say, *Forgive us our debts, as we also forgive our debtors.* And we are at work with out hands when we do this, *Break thy bread to the hungry, and bring the houseless poor into thine house.* (Isa. 58:7) *Shut up alms in the heart* *of a poor man, and it shall intercede for thee unto the Lord.* (Ecclus. 29:12)

Sermon 6, 11;
trans. Nicene, 6, 277.

152. Alms to the poor, which give great support to the prayers of widows, rather than gifts to the covetous find their way into the treasury of heaven. Fastings and vigils in so far as they do not injure health, if they are employed in prayer, in the singing of psalms, in reading, and in meditating on the law of God, even these very things that seem laborious, are changed into spiritual pleasures. The labors of those who love are never tiresome, but they are even a source of pleasure as in the case of hunters, fowlers, fishermen, grape harvesters, bankers, and persons who amuse themselves at some game. What matters is that the work be enjoyed. There is either no weariness in work that is loved, or the weariness itself is loved. If pleasure is found in such activities as capturing a wild animal, filling a cup or purse, or throwing a ball, think of the shame and grief we ought to feel if we do not find pleasure in the exercises for attaining God.

The Good of Widowhood for Juliana, 21, 26;
trans. FOC 16, 314-315.

XXIII. HUMILITY

153. But why should we wonder that He rose from supper, and laid aside His garments, who, being in the form of God, made Himself of no reputation? And why should we wonder, if He girded Himself with a towel, who took upon Him the form of a servant, and was found in the likeness of a man? (Phil. 2:6-7) Why wonder, if He poured water into a basin wherewith to wash His disciples' feet, who poured His blood upon the earth to wash away the filth of their sins? Why wonder, if with the towel wherewith He was girded He wiped the feet He had washed, who with the very flesh that clothed Him laid a firm pathway for the footsteps of His evangelists? In order, indeed, to gird Himself with the towel, He laid aside the garments He wore; but when He emptied Himself (of His divine glory) in order to assume the form of a servant, He laid not down what He had, but assumed that which He had not before.

On the Gospel of John, LV, 7;
trans. Nicene, 7, 301.

154. *Ye call me Lord and Master: and ye say well; for so I am. If I then, your Lord and Master, have washed your feet; how ought ye also to do* *to one another's feet?* (Jo. 13:13-15) If therefore strength is in humility, fear not the proud. The humble are like a rock: the rock seems to lie downwards: but nevertheless it is firm. What are the proud? Like smoke: although they are lofty, they vanish.

On Psalm 93, 3;
trans. Nicene, 8, 457.

155.   ...When ye hear sung in the Psalms, *Praise the Lord, ye children* (ver. 1); imagine not that that exhortation pertaineth not unto you, because having already passed the youth of the body, ye are either blooming in the prime of manhood, or growing gray with the honours of old age: for unto all of you the Apostle saith, *Brethren, be not children in understanding; howbeit, in malice be ye children, but in understanding be men.* (1 Cor. 14:20) What malice in particular, save pride? For it is pride that, presuming in false greatness, suffereth not man to walk along the narrow path, and to enter by the narrow gate; but the child easily entereth through the narrow entrance; and thus no man, save as a child, entereth into the kingdom of heaven.

On Psalm 113, 1;
trans. Nicene, 8, 548.

156.   ...*And plenteousness*, he addeth, *for them that love thee.* (ver. 6) He addresses Jerusalem herself, They have plenteousness who love her. Plenteousness after want: here they are destitute, there they are affluent; here they are weak, there they are strong; here they want, there they are rich. How have they become rich? Because they gave here what they received from God for a season, and received there what God will afterwards pay back for evermore. Here, my brethren, even rich men are poor. It is a good thing for a rich man to acknowledge himself poor: for if he think himself full, that is mere puffing, not plenteousness. Let him own himself empty, that he may be filled. What hath he? Gold. What hath he not yet? Everlasting life. Let him consider what he hath, and see what he hath not. Brethren, of that which he hath, let him give, that he may receive what he hath not; let him purchase out of that which he hath, that which he hath not, *and plenteousness for them that love thee.*

On Psalm 122, 11;
trans. Nicene, 8, 595.

157. *In the beginning was the Word, and the Word was with God, and the Word was God:* (Jo. 1:1) see what Mary was listening to! *The Word was made flesh, and dwelt among us:* (Jo. 1:14) see to whom Martha was ministering! Therefore *hath Mary chosen the better part, which shall not be taken from her.* For she chose that which shall abide for ever; *it shall not be taken from her.* She wished to be occupied about *one thing.* She understood already, *But it is good for me to cleave to the Lord.* (Ps. 73:28) She sat at the feet of our Head. The more lowly she sat, the more amply did she receive. For the water flows together to the low hollows of the valley, runs down from the risings of the hill. The Lord then did not blame Martha's work, but distinguished between their services. *Thou art occupied about many things; yet one thing is needful.* Already hath Mary chosen this for herself. The labour of manifoldness passeth away, and the love of unity abideth. Therefore what she hath chosen, *shall not be taken from her.* But from thee, that which thou hast chosen (of course this follows, of course this is understood) from thee, that which thou hast chosen shall be taken away. But to thy blessedness shall it be taken away, that that which is better may be given. For labour shall be taken away from thee, that rest may be given. Thou art still on the sea, she is already in port.

Sermon 54, 3;
trans. Nicene, 6, 429-430.

XXIV. CHRIST

158. And therefore I say, did Christ the Lord, made man, despise all the good things of earth, that He might show us that these things are to be despised; and endured all earthly ills that He taught must be endured; so that neither might happiness be sought in the former nor unhappiness be feared in the latter. For, in as much as He was born of a mother who, although she conceived, was untouched by man and always remained untouched, a virgin in conception, a virgin in childbearing, a virgin in death, was yet espoused to a workman, He put an end to all the inflated pride of carnal nobility. In as much as He was born, moreover, in the city of Bethlehem, which among all the cities of Judea was so insignificant, that even today it is called a village, He did not want any one to glory in the exaltation of an earthly city. He, likewise, became poor, to whom all things belong and by whom all things were created, lest anyone believing in Him should dare to be unduly exalted because of earthly riches. He refused to be made a king by men, because He was showing the way of lowliness to those wretches whom their pride had separated from Him; and yet the whole creation bears witness to His everlasting kingdom. He hungered who feeds all, He thirsted by whom all drink is created, He who is spiritually both the bread of them that hunger, and the well spring of them that thirst; He was wearied with earthly journeying who has made Himself the way to heaven for us; He became as it were one dumb and deaf in the presence of His revilers, through whom the dumb spoke and the deaf heard, He was bound who has freed men from the bonds of their infirmities; He was scourged who drove out from men's bodies the scourges of all pains; He was crucified who put an end to our torments; He died who raised the dead to life. But He also rose again, nevermore to die, that none might learn from Him so to despise death as though destined never to live hereafter.

On Catechizing the Uninstructed, 22, 40; trans. ACW 2, 71-72.

159. How did He come, except that *the Word was made flesh, and dwelt among us?* (1 Jo. 1:14) Just as in speaking: In order that what we have in our mind may penetrate to the mind of our listener through his ears of flesh, the word which we carry in our heart becomes a sound and is called speech. Nevertheless, our thought is not changed to the same sound. Remaining entire in itself, it takes on the nature of speech, by means of which it may penetrate his ears; yet it does not incur any deterioration in the change. Just so, the Word of

God, although unchanged, was made flesh, in order that He might dwell among us.

Christian Doctrine, I, 13;
trans. FOC 4, 36.

160. How great the difference, when two are in a prison, between the criminal and him that visits him! For upon a time a person comes to his friend and enters in to visit him, and both seem to be in prison; but they differ by a wide distinction. The one, his cause presses down: the other, humanity has brought thither. So in this our mortal state, we were held fast by our guiltiness, He in mercy came down: He entered in unto the captive, a Redeemer not an oppressor. The Lord for us shed His blood, redeemed us, changed our hope. As yet we bear the mortality of the flesh, and take the future immortality upon trust: and on the sea we are tossed by the waves, but we have the anchor of hope already fixed upon the land.

Epistle of John to the Parthians, II, 10;
trans. Nicene, 7, 473.

161. *Because all that is in the world is the desire of the flesh, and the desire of the eyes, and the pretensions of this life*—three things, *which are not of the Father but of the world. And the world passeth away, and the desires thereof; but he that doeth the will of God abideth for ever, as he abideth for ever.*

Why may I not love what God has made? Make your choice: either to love things temporal and pass away with time's passing, or not to love the world, and to live for ever with God. The river of time sweeps us on; but there, like a tree growing by the river, is our Lord Jesus Christ. He took flesh, died, rose again, ascended into heaven. He willed to plant himself as it were beside the river of things temporal. If you are drifting down to the rapids, lay hold of the tree: if you are caught up in the world's love, lay hold of Christ. He for your sake entered into time, that you might win eternity; for by his entering into time he did not cease himself to be eternal.

Epistle of John to the Parthians, II, 10; trans. Burnaby, 275.

162. He that praises God with his tongue, cannot be always doing this: he that by his life and conduct praises God, can be doing it always. Works of mercy, affections of charity, sanctity of piety, incorruptness of chastity, modesty of sobriety, these things are always to be practiced: whether we are in public, or at home; whether before men, or in our chamber; whether speaking, or holding our peace; whether occupied upon something, or free from occupation: these are always to be kept, because all these virtues which I have named are within. But who is sufficient to name them all? There is as it were the army of an emperor seated within in thy mind. For as an emperor by his army does what he will, so the

Lord Jesus Christ, once beginning to dwell in our inner man, (*i.e.* in the mind through faith), uses these virtues as His ministers. And by these virtues which cannot be seen with eyes, and yet when they are named are praised—and they would not be praised except they were loved, not loved except they were seen; and if not loved except seen, they are seen with another eye, that is, with the inward beholding of the heart—by these invisible virtues, the members are visibly put in motion: the feet to walk, but whither? whither they are moved by the good will which as a soldier serves the good emperor: the hands to work; but what? that which is bidden by charity which is inspired within by the Holy Ghost. The members then are seen when they are put in motion; He that orders them within is not seen: and who He is that orders them within is known almost alone to Him that orders, and to him who within is ordered.

Epistle of John to the Parthians, VIII, 1; trans. Nicene, 7, 506.

163. God has no need of servants, but servants have need of God. Hence the words of the Psalm: *I have said unto the Lord, thou art my God*—yes, God is the true Lord—*because thou needest not my goods.* (Ps. 16:2) You need the good your servant provides. He needs the good you provide for him in feeding him, and you need the good he provides for you by his service. For yourself you cannot do all the drawing of water, the cooking, the running before your carriage, the grooming of your beast. You are in want of the good your servant furnishes, you are in want of his attendance; and inasmuch as you want an inferior, you are no true lord. The true lord is he who seeks nothing from us; and it goes ill with us, if we seek not him. He seeks nothing from us, yet he sought us when we were not seeking him. One sheep had gone astray: he found it and brought it home upon his shoulders rejoicing. (Luke 15:4) Was the sheep a necessity for the shepherd, or not rather the shepherd a necessity for the sheep?

Epistle of John to the Parthians, VIII, 14; trans. Burnaby, p. 327.

164.   On this occasion the Lord made appropriate mention of what Jacob saw in his dream: *Verily I say unto you, Ye shall see heaven opened, and the angels of God ascending and descending upon the Son of man.* (Jo. 1:47-51) This Jacob saw, who in the blessing was called Israel, when he had the stone for a pillow, and had the vision of the ladder reaching from earth to heaven, on which the angels of God were ascending and descending. (Gen. 28:11-18) The angels denote the evangelists, or preachers of Christ. They ascend when they rise above the created universe to describe the supreme majesty of the divine nature of Christ as being in the beginning God with God, by whom all things were made. They descend to tell of His being made of a woman, made under the law, that He might redeem them that were under the law. Christ is the ladder reaching from earth to heaven, or from the carnal to the spiritual: for by His assistance the carnal ascended to spirituality; and the spiritual may be said to descend to nourish the carnal with milk when they cannot speak to them as to spiritual, but as to carnal. (1 Cor. 3:1-3) There is thus both an ascent and a descent upon the Son of man. For the Son of man is above as our head, being Himself the Savior; and He is below in His body, the Church. He is the ladder, for He says, *I am the way.* We ascend to Him to see Him in heavenly places; we descend to Him for the nourishment of His weak members. And the ascent and descent are by Him as well as to Him.

Against Faustus the Manichee, XII, 26;
trans. Nicene, 4, 192.

165. For if in language the form of the verb changes in the number of letters and syllables according to the tense, as *done* signifies the past, and *to be done* the future, why should not the symbols which declare Christ's death and resurrection to be accomplished, differ from those which predicted their accomplishment, as we see a difference in the form and sound of the words, past and future, suffered and to suffer, risen and to rise? For material symbols are nothing else than visible speech, which, though sacred, is changeable and transitory. For while God is eternal, the water of baptism, and all that is material in the sacrament, is transitory: the very word *God*, which must be pronounced in the consecration, is a sound which passes in a moment. The actions and sounds pass away, but their efficacy remains the same, and the spiritual gift thus communicated is eternal. To say, therefore, that if Christ had not destroyed the law and the prophets, the sacraments of the law and the prophets would continue to be observed in the congregations of the Christian Church, is the same as to say that if Christ had not destroyed the law and the prophets, He would still be predicted as about to be born, to suffer, and to rise again; whereas, in fact, it is proved that He did not destroy, but fulfill those things, because the prophecies of His birth, and passion, and resurrection, which were represented in these ancient sacraments, have ceased, and the sacraments now observed by Christians contain the announcement that He has been born, has suffered, has risen.

Against Faustus the Manichee, XIX, 16; trans. Nicene, 4, 244-245.

166. Augustine replied: You understand neither the symbols of the law nor the acts of the prophets, because you do not know what holiness or righteousness means. We have repeatedly shown, at great length, that the precepts and symbols of the Old Testament contained both what was to be fulfilled in obedience through the grace bestowed in the New Testament, and what was to be set aside as a proof of its having been fulfilled in the truth now made manifest. For in the love of God and of our neighbor is secured the accomplishment of the precepts of the law, while the accomplishment of its promises is shown in the abolition of circumcision, and of other typical observances formerly practised. By the precept men were led, through a sense of guilt, to desire salvation; by the promise they were led to find in the typical observances the assurance that the Savior would come. The salvation desired was to be obtained through the grace bestowed on the appearance of the New Testament; and the fulfillment of the expectation rendered the types no longer necessary. The same law that was given by Moses became grace and truth in Jesus Christ. By the grace in the pardon of sin, the precept is kept in force in the case of those supported by divine help. By the truth the symbolic rites are set aside, that the promise might, in those who trust in the divine faithfulness, be brought to pass.

Those, accordingly, who, finding fault with what they do not understand, call the typical institutions of the law disfigurements and excrescences, are like men displeased with things of which they do not know the use. As if a deaf man, seeing others move their lips in speaking, were to find fault with the motion of the mouth as needless and unsightly; or as if a blind man, on hearing a house commended, were to test the truth of what he heard by passing his hand over the surface of the wall, and on coming to the windows were to cry out against them as flaws in the level, or were to suppose that the wall had fallen in.

Against Faustus the Manichee, XXII, 6-7; trans. Nicene, 4, 274.

167. Thus, when the very passages on which the heretics found their objections to the Scriptures are studied and examined, the more obscure they are the more wonderful are the secrets which we discover in reply to our questions; so that the mouths of blasphemers are completely stopped, and the evidence of the truth so stifles them that they cannot even utter a sound. The unhappy men who will not receive into their hearts the sweetness of the truth must feel its force as a gag in their mouths. All those passages speak of Christ. The head now ascended into heaven along with the body still suffering on earth is the full development of the whole purpose of the authors of Scripture, which is well called Sacred Scripture. Every part of the narrative in the prophetical books should be viewed as having a figurative meaning, except what serves merely as a framework for the literal or figurative predictions of this king and of his people. For as in harps and other musical instruments the musical sound does not come from all parts of the instrument, but from the strings, and the rest is only for fastening and stretching the strings so as to tune them, that when they are struck by the musician they may give a pleasant sound; so in these prophetical narratives the circumstances selected by the prophetic spirit either predict some future event, or if they have no voice of their own, they serve to connect together other significant utterances.

Against Faustus the Manichee, XXII, 94;
trans. Nicene, 4, 310-311.

168. *In the beginning was the Word.* He is the same, and is in the same manner; as He is, so He is always; He cannot be changed; that is, he *is*. This His name He spoke to His servant Moses: *I am that I am; and He that is hath sent me.* (Ex. 3:14) Who then shall comprehend this when you see that all mortal things are variable; when you see that not only do bodies vary as to their qualities, by being born, by increasing, by becoming less, by dying, but that even souls themselves through the effect of divers volitions are distended and divided; when you see that men can obtain wisdom if they apply themselves to its light and heat, and also lose wisdom if they remove themselves from it through some evil influence? When, therefore, you see that all those things are variable, what is that which is, unless that which transcends all things which are so that they are not? Who then can receive this? Or who, in what manner soever he may have applied the strength of his mind to touch that which is, can reach to that which he may in any way have touched with his mind? It is as if one were to see his native land at a distance, and the sea intervening; he sees whither he would go, but he has not the means of going. So we desire to arrive at that our stability where that which is, is, because this alone always is as it is: the sea of the world interrupts our course, even although we see whither we go; for many do not even see whither they go. That there might be a way by which we could go, He has come from Him to whom we wished to go. And what has He done? He has appointed a tree by which we may cross the sea. For no one is able to cross the sea of this world, unless borne by the cross of Christ. Even he who is of weak eyesight sometimes embraces this cross; and he who does not see from afar whither he goes, let him not depart from it, and it will carry him over.

On the Gospel of John, II, 2;
trans. Nicene, 7, 14.

169. But let them not suppose that it is not of Christ it is spoken when it is said, *God reigned over all the earth.* For who else is our King, but our Lord Jesus Christ? It is He that is our King. And what have you heard in the same psalm, in the verse just sung? *Sing praises to our God, sing praises: sing praises to our King, sing praises.* Whom he called God, the same he called our King: *Sing praises to our God, sing praises: sing praises to our King, sing ye praises with understanding.* And that thou shouldest not understand Him to whom thou singest praises to reign in one part, he says, *For God is King of all the earth.* (Ps. 47·8) And how is He king of all the earth, who appeared in one part of the earth, in Jerusalem, in Judea, walking among men, born, sucking the breast, growing, eating, drinking, waking, sleeping, sitting at a well, wearied; laid hold of, scourged, spat upon, crowned with thorns, hanged on a tree, wounded with a spear, dead, buried? How then King of all the earth? What was seen locally was flesh, to carnal eyes only flesh was visible; the immortal majesty was concealed in mortal flesh. And with what eyes shall we be able to behold the immortal majesty, after penetrating through the structure of the flesh? There is another eye, there is an inner eye. Tobias, for example, was not without eyes; when, blind in his bodily eyes, he was giving precepts of life to his son. The son was holding the father's hand, that the father might walk with his feet, whilst the father was giving the son counsel to walk in the way of righteousness. Here I see eyes, and there I understand eyes. And better are the eyes of him that gives counsel of life, than his who holds the hand. Such eyes Jesus also required when He said to Philip, *Am I so long time with you, and ye have not known me?* Such eyes He required when he said, *Philip, he that seeth me, seeth the Father.* These are the eyes of the understanding, these are the eyes of the mind.

On the Gospel of John, XIII, 3; trans. Nicene, 7, 87.

170. Thou holdest out a green twig to a sheep, and thou drawest it. Nuts are shown to a child, and he is attracted; he is drawn by what he runs to, drawn by loving it, drawn without hurt to the body, drawn by a cord of the heart. If, then, these things, which among earthly delights and pleasures are shown to them that love them, draw them, since it is true that *every man is drawn by his own pleasure*, does not Christ, revealed by the Father, draw? For what does the soul more strongly desire than the truth? For what ought it to have a greedy appetite, with which to wish that there may be within a healthy palate for judging the things that are true, unless it be to eat and drink wisdom, righteousness, truth, eternity?

On the Gospel of John, XXVI, 5;
trans. Nicene, 7, 170.

171. *No man has ascended into heaven, but He who came down from heaven, the Son of man who is in heaven.* (Jo. 3:13) He said not, who *was* in heaven. He spoke on the earth, and declared that He was at the same time in heaven. He came in such wise that He departed not thence; and He so returned as not to abandon us. What do ye marvel at? This is God's doing. For man, as regards his body, is in a place, and departs from a place; and when he comes to another place, he will not be in that place whence he came: but God fills all things, and is all everywhere; He is not held in places according to space. Nevertheless the Lord Christ was, as regards His visible flesh, on the earth: as regards His invisible majesty, He was in heaven and on earth; and therefore He says, *Where I am , thither ye cannot come.* Nor did He say, *Ye shall not be able,* but, *ye are not* *able to come;* for at that time they were such as were not able.

On the Gospel of John, XXXI, 9;
trans. Nicene, 7, 191-192.

172.   You see, then, my brethren, you see, if you see inwardly, what kind of light this is, of which the Lord says, *He that followeth me shall not walk in darkness.* Follow the sun, and let us see if thou wilt not walk in darkness. Behold, by rising it comes forth to thee; it goes by its course towards the west. Perhaps thy journey is towards the east: unless thou goest in a contrary direction to that in which it travels, thou wilt certainly err by following it, and instead of east wilt get to the west. If thou follow it by land, thou wilt go wrong; if the mariner follow it by sea, he will go wrong. Finally, it seems to thee, suppose, that thou must follow the sun, and thou also travellest thyself towards the west, whither it also travels; let us see after it has set if thou wilt not walk in darkness. See how, although thou art not willing to desert it, yet it will desert thee, to finish the day by necessity of its service. But our Lord Jesus Christ, even when He was not manifest to all through the cloud of His flesh, was yet at the same time holding all things by the power of His wisdom. Thy God is whole everywhere: if thou fall not off from Him, He will never fall away from thee.

On the Gospel of John, XXXIV, 6;
trans. Nicene, 7, 201-202.

173. ...I have done this, and God has spared me; I have committed this, and He hath borne with me; I have heard the gospel, and despised it; I have been baptized, and returned again to the same course: what am I doing? whither am I going? how shall I escape? When thou speakest thus, Christ is already groaning; for thy faith is groaning. In the voice of one who groaneth thus, there comes to light the hope of his rising again. If such faith is within, there is Christ groaning; for if there is faith in us, Christ is in us. For what else says the apostle: *That Christ may dwell in your hearts by faith.* (Eph. 3:17) Therefore thy faith in Christ is Christ Himself in thy heart. This is why He slept in the ship; and why, when His disciples were in danger and already on the verge of shipwreck, they came to Him and awoke Him. Christ arose, laid His commands on the winds and waves, and there ensured a great calm. (Matt. 8:24-26) So also with thee; the winds enter thy heart, that is, where thou sailest, where thou passest along this life as a stormy and dangerous sea; the winds enter, the billows rise and toss thy vessel. What are the winds? Though hast received some insult, and art wroth: that insult is the wind; that anger, the waves. Thou art in danger, thou preparest to reply, to render cursing for cursing, and thy vessel is already nigh to shipwreck. Awake the Christ who is sleeping. For thou art in commotion, and making ready to render evil for evil, because Christ is sleeping in thy vessel. For the sleep of Christ in thy heart is the forgetfulness of faith. But if thou arousest Christ, that is, recallest thy faith, what dost thou hear said to thee by Christ, when now awake in thy heart? I (He says) Have heard it said to me, *Thou hast a devil*, (Matt. 7:30) and I have prayed for them. The Lord hears and suffers; the servant hears and is angry! But thou wishest to be avenged. Why so? I am already avenged. When thy faith so speaks to thee, command is exercised, as it were, over the winds and waves, and there is a great calm. As, then, to awaken Christ in the vessel is just to awaken faith; so in the heart of one who is pressed down by a great mass and habit of sin, in the heart of the man who has been a transgressor even of the holy gospel and a despiser of eternal punishment, let Christ groan, let such a man betake himself to self-accusation.

On the Gospel of John, XLIX, 19;
trans. Nicene, 7, 276.

174. *Hosanna: blessed is He that cometh in the name of the Lord, the King of Israel.* What a cross of mental suffering must the Jewish rulers have endured when they heard so great a multitude proclaiming Christ as their King! But what honor was it to the Lord to be King of Israel? What great thing was it to the King of eternity to become the King of men? For Christ's kingship over Israel was not for the purpose of exacting tribute, of putting swords into His soldiers' hands, of subduing His enemies by open warfare;

but He was King of Israel in exercising kingly authority over their inward natures, in consulting for their eternal interests, in bringing into His heavenly kingdom those whose faith, and hope, and love were centered in Himself. Accordingly, for the Son of God, the Father's equal, the Word by whom all things were made, in His good pleasure to be King of Israel, was an act of condescension and not of promotion; a token of compassion, and not any increase of power. For He who was called on earth the King of the Jews, is in the heavens the Lord of angels.

On the Gospel of John, LI, 4; trans. Nicene, , , 284.

175. Accordingly, brethren, when you hear the Lord saying, *Where I am, there shall also my servant be,* do not think merely of good bishops and clergymen. But be yourselves also in your own way serving Christ, by good lives, by giving alms, by preaching His name and doctrine as you can; and every father of a family also, be acknowledging in this name the affection he owes as a parent to his family. For Christ's sake, and for the sake of eternal life, let him be warning, and teaching, and exhorting, and correcting all his household; let him show kindliness, and exercise discipline; and so in his own house he will be filling an ecclesiastical and kind of episcopal office, and serving Christ, that he may be with Him forever.

On the Gospel of John, LI, 13; trans. Nicene, 7, 286-287.

176. And if we turn our thoughts even to the most blessed apostles, we find that he who labored more than they all, yet not he, but the grace of God that was with him, (1 Cor. 15:10) besought the Lord thrice that the messenger of Satan might depart from him, and received not what he had asked. (2 Cor. 12:8) What shall we say, beloved? Are we to suppose that the promise here made, *Whatsoever ye shall ask in my name, I will do it,* was not fulfilled by Him even to the apostles? And to whom, then, will ever His promise be fulfilled, if therein He has deceived His own apostles?

Wake up, then, believer, and give careful heed to what is stated here, *in my name*: for in these words He does not say, *whatsoever ye shall ask* in any way; but, *in my name.* How, then, is He called, who promised so great a blessing? Christ Jesus, of course: Christ means King, and Jesus means Saviour! for certainly it is not any one who is a king that will save us, but only the Saviour-King; and therefore, whatsoever we ask that is adverse to the interests of salvation, we do not ask in the name of the Saviour. And yet He is the Saviour, not only when He does what we ask, but also when He refuses to do so; since by not doing what He sees to be contrary to our salvation, He manifests Himself the more fully as our Saviour. For the physician knows which of his patient's requests will be favorable, and which will be adverse, to his safety; and therefore yields not to his wishes when asking what is prejudicial, that he may effect his recovery. Accordingly, when we wish Him to do whatsoever we ask, let it not be in any way, but in His name, that is, in the name of the Saviour, that we present our petition.

On the Gospel of John, LXXIII, 2-3;
trans. Nicene, 7, 332.

177. And although Christ would not have been the vine had He not been man, yet He could not have supplied such grace to the branches had He not also been God.

On the Gospel of John, LXXXI, 3;
trans. Nicene, 7, 346.

178. If you are stirred by the fact that no other star but the sun gives light to our day, who, I ask you, appeared so great to men, as the Man whom God received far otherwise that He does the rest of saints and wise men? If you compare Him with other men, they are separated by a greater distance than are the other stars in comparison with the sun.

Letter 14, to Nebridius;
trans. FOC 9, 34.

179. Therefore, we need have no fear about that tiny body of infancy, that so great a God should seem to be confined in it. God's greatness is not in mass but in power; He has given a greater sense of foresight to tiny ants and bees than to asses and camels; He creates the immense spread of the fig tree from the smallest seed, while many much smaller things grow from much larger seeds; He has endowed the minute pupil of the eye with the power of sight by which in an instant it sweeps across almost half the sky; He has centered all the senses in one spot of the brain, and from there sends out their fivefold activity; He radiates the lifegiving impulse through all the parts of the body from the heart, an organ of insignificant size: in these and other like instances, He who is not small in small things produces great things from the least. For, that very greatness of His power, which feels no narrowness in narrow quarters, enriched the Virgin's womb, not by an externally caused but by an instrinsic childbirth; that power took to itself a rational soul and thereby also a human body, and chose to better all mankind without suffering any diminution itself, deigning to take the name of humanity from man, while granting him a share in the divinity. That same power brought forth the body of the infant from the inviolate virginal womb of the mother, as afterward the Body of the Man penetrated closed doors. (Jo. 20:19-26) It will not be wondered at if an explanation is asked of this; it will not be remarkable if an example is demanded. Let us grant that God can do something which we confess we cannot fathom. In such matters the whole explanation of the deed is in the power of the doer.

Letter 137, to Volusian;
trans. FOC 11, 23-24.

180. Where would that stream of the repulsive malice of the human race not have carried us, who would not have been swept along with it, in what depths would it not have overwhelmed us, if the cross of Christ had not been planted, firm and high, in the great rock of authority, so that we might take hold of its strength and be steadied, and might not be drawn under the vast current of the ruined world by listening to evil advisers, urging us to evil? For, in the midst of that filth of depraved morals, and of an ancient decadent learning, it was eminently right for a heavenly authority to come and to bring relief by counseling voluntary poverty, chastity, kindness, justice, concord, true filial love, and those other virtues which are the light and strength of life, not only to make us lead this life with the utmost regard for honor, nor only for the sake of making the society of the earthly çity as united as possible, but also that we may attain salvation and reach that heavenly and divine country, whose peoples are immortal.

Letter 138, to Marcellinus; trans. FOC 11, 49-50.

181. Thus, the man Christ was not to be recommended to us by reason of earthly happiness, because by Him the grace of the New Testament was to be revealed, which belongs to eternal not to temporal life. Hence, subjection, suffering, scourging, being spat upon, contempt, the cross, wounds, and death itself were to be His, as if He had been overcome and made prisoner by them, so that His faithful might learn what reward for their devotion they should ask and hope for from Him whose sons they had become, and might not serve God for the purpose of seeking to gain temporal happiness as a great boon, and by so serving Him should cast away and trample on their faith, rating it as a cheap reward. Hence, almighty God, by a most bountiful providence, granted earthly happiness to the wicked so that the good might not seek it as a great boon.

Letter 140, 5 to Honoratus; trans. FOC 11, 67.

182. To acquire humility, repeat the following: (ver. 3) *In the Lord shall my soul be praised; let the meek hear and rejoice.* Those, I say, who wish to be praised but not in the Lord are not meek, but rough and rude, arrogant and proud. Our Lord would have meek beasts to ride upon: you must be our Lord's mount, that is, you must be meek. He sits upon you, He governs you: do not be afraid of stumbling and falling headlong. The weakness is your own, but consider who it is that controls you. You may be the ass's colt, but you are bearing Christ. For He rode into the city on the ass's colt, and it proved a gentle mount. Was the beast ever praised? Was it to the beast they sang: *Hosanna to the Son of David; blessed is He that cometh in the name of the Lord?* (Matt. 21:9) The ass-colt carried Him: but it was He that was carried who received the acclamations of those that went before and those that followed. And perhaps the beast said: *In the Lord shall my soul be praised; let the meek hear and rejoice.* Brethren, the ass never spoke like this; but the people who imitate that beast of burden must say it if they wish to carry the weight of their Lord. Possibly people are ruffled at being compared to the ass-colt on which our Lord rode; and some proud folk will say to me in contempt: *Why, he is making asses of us!* Very well; let whoever says that become our Lord's ass, for fear of becoming the horse and the mule devoid of understanding. For you know the Psalm in which it is said: *Do not become like the horse and the mule, who have no understanding.* (Ps. 31:9) The horse and mule sometimes uprear their necks and throw their riders out of sheer ferocity. They are tamed with bit and bridle and blows, until they learn to submit and carry their master. But before your jaws are bruised with the bit, be meek and carry your Lord. Do not seek praise for yourself, seek it rather for Him who rides you. *In the Lord shall my soul be praised,* you must say; *let the meek hear and rejoice.*

On Psalm 33, Serm. 2, 5; trans. ACW 30, 161-162.

183. He saw His own betrayer, and chose him as the more necessary to His work. Through that man's evil He wrought a great good; and yet He was chosen among the Twelve, so that not even so small a number as a dozen should be without one bad member. This was to set us an example of patience, for we have to live among the wicked; we have to bear with wicked men, whether we recognize them or not. He set an example of patience so that you may not fail when you come to live among miscreants. And since that group of Christ's followers, the Twelve, did not end with them, how much more ought we to be steadfast, now that what was foretold about the intermingling of the wicked is fulfilled in the Church at large?

On Psalm 34, Serm. 1, 10;
trans. ACW 30, 198.

184. *Thy justice is as the mountains of God, thy judgments are a great deep.* (ver. 7) Who are God's mountains? We have just termed clouds those who are the mountains of God; for the great preachers are God's mountains. Just as the sun in its rising first clothes the mountains with light, and afterwards the light descends to the lowest levels of the earth, so when our Lord Jesus Christ came, He first shone upon the lofty height of the apostles, He first illumined the mountains, and thus His light came down to the secluded valley of the world. And therefore we find in a certain passage in a Psalm: *I have lifted up my eyes to the mountains, from whence help shall come to me.* (Ps. 120:1) Do not suppose, however, that the mountains themselves will afford you help: whatever they give, they receive; they do not give of themselves. And if you stay on the mountains, your hope will not be unshakable: your hope and confidence must be rather in Him who shed light upon the mountains, because the Scriptures have been consigned to you through the mountains, by the great preachers of the truth; but do not set your hope in them.

On Psalm 35, 9;
trans. ACW 30, 233-234.

185. *By the Lord shall the steps of a man be directed; and he shall like well His way.* (ver. 23) As I began by saying, if you wish for Christ's way, if you are a true Christian, and the true Christian is one who does not scorn the way of Christ but wishes to follow it through his sufferings, seek to go by no other road than that by which He went. It may seem a rough road but it is a safe one; the other possibly has its delights but it swarms with robbers. *And he shall like well His way.*

When he shall fall he shall not be distressed, for the Lord strengtheneth his hand. (ver. 24) Notice what delight in Christ's way implies. Should a man happen to suffer some trial, some disgrace, some outrage, some affliction, some injury, or one of the many evils to which human nature is heir in this life, he sets his own Lord before his eyes, he reflects upon the multitude of His trials and sufferings; *when he shall fall, therefore, he shall not be disturbed, for the Lord,* who has suffered before him, *strengtheneth his hand*. For what have you to fear, man, when your steps are so directed as to lead you to delight in the way of the Lord? What have you to fear? Physical pain? Christ was scourged. (Matt. 27:26) Insolence? He was told: *Thou hast a devil*, (Jo. 8:48) He who was casting them out. Or possibly you fear intrigue and the plots of wicked men? They plotted against Him. (Jo. 9:22) Perhaps you are unable to prove that your conscience is clear on the score of some accusation, and you are forced to suffer because the evidence of false witnesses is accepted against you. They bore false witness against Him in the first place, not only before His death but also after His resurrection. (Matt. 26:60)

On Psalm 36, Serm. 2, 16-17; trans. ACW 30, 286.

186. The sea was raging, the bark wherein the disciples were sailing was being tossed; but Christ was sleeping: at length it was seen by them that among them was sleeping the Ruler and Creator of winds; they drew near and awoke Christ; (Matt. 8:24-25) He commanded the winds, and there was a great calm. With reason then perchance thy heart is troubled, because thou hast forgotten Him on whom thou hast believed: beyond endurance thou art suffering, because it hath not come into thy mind what for thee Christ hath borne. If unto thy mind cometh not Christ,

He sleepeth: awake Christ, recall faith. For then in thee Christ is sleeping, if thou hast forgotten the sufferings of Christ: then in thee Christ is watching, if thou hast remembered the sufferings of Christ. But when with full heart thou shalt have considered what He hath suffered, wilt not thou too with equanimity endure? and perchance rejoicing, because thou hast been found in some likeness of the sufferings of thy King. When therefore on these things thinking thou has begun to be comforted and to rejoice, He hath arisen, He hath commanded the winds; therefore there is a great calm.

On Psalm 55,9;
trans. Nicene, 8, 212.

187. *Thou hast led me down, because Thou hast been made my hope: a tower of strength from the face of the enemy.* (ver. 3) My heart is vexed, saith that Unity from the ends of the earth, and I toil amid temptations and offences: the heathen envy, because they have been conquered; the heretics lie in wait, hidden in the cloak of the Christian name: within in the Church itself the wheat suffereth violence from the chaff: amid all these things when my heart is vexed, I will cry from the ends of the earth. But there forsaketh me not the Same that hath exalted me upon the Rock, in order to lead me down even unto Himself, because even if I labour, while the devil through so many places and times and occasions lieth in wait against me, He is to me a tower of strength, to whom when I shall have fled for refuge, not only I shall escape the weapons of the enemy, but even against him securely I shall myself hurl whatever darts I shall please. For Christ Himself is the tower, Himself for us hath been made a tower from the face of the enemy, who is also the Rock whereon hath been builded the Church. Art thou taking heed that thou be not smitten of the devil? Flee to the tower; never to that tower will the devil's darts follow thee: there thou wilt stand protected and fixed.

On Psalm 61, 4;
trans. Nicene, 8, 249.

188. *That hath turned the sea into dry land. In the river they shall pass over on foot.* (ver. 6) Those same persons that have been turned into dry land, though they were before sea, *in the river on foot shall pass over.* What is the river? The river is all the mortality of the world. Observe a river: some things come and pass by, other things that are to pass by do succeed. Is it not thus with the water of a river, that from earth springeth and floweth? Every one that is born must needs give place to one going to be born: and all this order of things rolling along is a kind of river. Into this river let not the soul greedily throw herself, let her not throw herself, but let her stand still. And how shall she pass over the pleasures of things doomed to perish? Let her believe in Christ, and she will pass over on foot:

she passeth over with Him for Leader, on foot she passeth over.

On Psalm 66, 9;
trans. Nicene, 8, 277.

189. ...*My soul is exceeding sorrowful, even unto death.* (Matt. 26:37-38) The Prophet who composed this Psalm, foreseeing that this would happen, introduces Him saying, *My soul is full of evils, and My life draweth nigh unto hell.* For the very same sense is here expressed in other words, as when He said, *My soul is sorrowful, even unto death.* The words, *My soul is sorrowful*, are like these, *My soul is full of evils:* and what follows, *even unto death*, like, *my life draweth nigh unto hell.* These feelings of human infirmity our Lord took upon Him, as He did the flesh of human infirmity, and the death of human flesh, not by the necessity of His condition, but by the free will of His mercy, that He might transfigure unto Himself His own body, which is the Church (the head of which He deigned to be), that is, His members in His holy and faithful disciples: that if amid human temptations any one among them happened to be in sorrow and pain, he might not therefore think that he was separated from His favour: that the body, like the chorus following its leader, might learn from its Head, that these sorrows were not sin, but proofs of human weakness.

On Psalm 88, 3;
trans. Nicene, 8, 424-425.

190. *O Lord, how glorious are Thy works: Thy thoughts are made very deep.* (ver. 5) Verily, my brethren, there is no sea so deep as these thoughts of God, who maketh the wicked flourish, and the good suffer: nothing so profound, nothing so deep: therein every unbelieving soul is wrecked, in that depth, in that profundity. Dost thou wish to cross this depth? Remove not from the wood of Christ's Cross: thou shalt not sink: hold thyself fast to Christ. What do I mean by this, hold fast to Christ? It was for this reason that He chose to suffer on earth Himself. Ye have heard, while the prophet was being read, how He *did not turn away His back from the smiters, and His face from the spittings of men, how He turned not His cheek from their hands;* (Isa. 50:6) wherefore chose He to suffer all these things, but that He might console the suffering? He could have raised His flesh at the last day: but then thou wouldest not have had thy ground of hope, since thou hadst not seen Him. He deferred not His resurrection, that thou mightest not still be in doubt. Suffer then tribulation in the world with the same end as that which thou hast observed in Christ: and let not those who do evil, and flourish in this life, move thee.

On Psalm 92, 8;
trans. Nicene, 8, 454.

191. An adulterous woman is brought forward to be stoned according to the Law, but she is brought before the Lawgiver Himself...Our Lord, at the time she was brought before Him, bending His Head, began writing on the earth. When He bent Himself down upon the earth, He then wrote on the earth: before He bent upon the earth, He wrote not on the earth, but on stone. The earth was now something fertile, ready to bring forth from the Lord's letters. On the stone He had written the Law, intimating the hardness of the Jews: He wrote on the earth, signifying the productiveness of Christians. Then they who were leading the adulteress came, like raging waves against a rock: but they were dashed to pieces by His answer. For He said to them, *He that is without sin among you, let him first cast a stone at her* (Jo. 8:7)

On Psalm 103, 9;
trans. Nicene, 8, 506.

192. And if it is beaten by the waves, yet it breaketh the waves, is not broken by them: this is the excellency of the rock in the sea. How great waves beat on our Lord Jesus Christ? The Jews dashed against Him; they were broken, He remained whole. And let every one who doth imitate Christ, so dwell in this world, that is, in this sea, where he cannot but feel storms and tempests, that he may yield to no wind, to no wave, but remain whole, while he meets them all.

On Psalm 104, 24;
trans. Nicene, 8, 515.

193. *He shall drink of the brook in the way, therefore shall he lift up his head.* (ver. 7) Let us consider Him drinking of the brook in the way: first of all, what is the brook? the onward flow of human mortality: for as a brook is gathered together by the rain, overflows, roars, runs, and by running runs down, that is, finishes its course; so is all this course of mortality. Men are born, they live, they die, and when some die others are born, and when they die others are born, they succeed, they flock together, they depart and will not remain. What is held fast here? what doth not run? what is not on its way to the abyss as if it was gathered together from rain? For as a river suddenly drawn together from rain from the drops of showers runneth into the sea, and is seen no more, nor was it seen before it was collected from the rain; so this hidden rain is collected together from hidden sources, and floweth on; at death again it travelleth where it is hidden: this intermediate state soundeth and passeth away. Of this brook He drinketh, He hath not disdained to drink of this brook; for to drink of this brook was to Him to be born and to die. What this brook hath, is birth and death; Christ assumed this, He was born, he died. *Therefore hath He lifted up His head*; that is, because He was humble, and *became obedient unto death, even the death of the Cross: therefore God also hath highly exalted Him, and given Him a Name which is above every name; that at the Name of Jesus every knee shall* *bow, of things in Heaven, and things in earth, and things under the earth; and that every tongue shall confess that Jesus Christ the Lord is in the glory of God the Father.* (Philip. 2:8-11)

On Psalm 110, 14;
trans. Nicene, 8, 544.

194. *Halleluia. Praise the Lord,* thou sayest to thy neighbour, he to thee: when all are exhorting each other, all are doing what they exhort others to do. But praise with your whole selves: that is, let not your tongue and voice alone praise God, but your conscience also, your life, your deeds. For now, when we are gathered together in the Church, we praise: when we go forth each to his own business, we seem to cease to praise God. Let a man not cease to live well, and then he ever praiseth God...It is impossible for a man's acts to be evil, whose thoughts are good. For acts issue from thought: nor can a man do anything or move his limbs to do aught, unless the bidding of his thought precede: just as in all things which ye see done throughout the provinces, whatsoever the Emperor biddeth goeth forth from the inner part of his palace throughout the whole Roman Empire. How great commotion is caused at one bidding by the Emperor as he sits in his palace! He but moveth his lips, when he speaketh: the whole province is moved, when what he speaketh is being executed. So in each single man too, the Emperor is within, his seat is in the heart. If he be good and biddeth good things, good things are done: if he be bad and biddeth evil things, evil things are done. When Christ sitteth there, what can He bid, but what is good? When the devil is the occupant, what can he bid, but evil? But God hath willed that it should be in thy choice for whom thou wilt prepare room, for God, or for the devil: when thou hast prepared it, he who is occupant will also rule. Therefore, brethren, attend not only to the sound; when ye praise God, praise with your whole selves: let your voice, your life, your deeds, all sing.

On Psalm 148, 2;
trans. Nicene, 8, 673-674.

195. All human beings are created by the one God, the Creator. We are not surprised that through the evil acts of human beings, God performs good deeds. Through Judas' betrayal Christ saved the human race. Notice that when God performs good deeds through the evil acts of human beings, frequently the sinner doesn't will the good results. There is a twofold distinction between the way the sinner sins and God acts. First of all, the intention of the sinner sinning differs from the intention of God effecting salvation through the sin—Judas' intention differed from Christ's intention allowing Himself to be betrayed. Secondly, their intentions also differ because the sinner is sad rather than joyful when he sees his sin resulting in a good he doesn't want. It is like someone wishing to poison a sick enemy by mistake administers medicine to him with the result that the sick man regains his health through the goodness of God who willed to turn the evil act of the sinner to the advantage of the sick person. When he sees that his action has effected the cure of his ailing enemy, the sinner would surely be saddened.

Sermon 10;
trans. Brady.

196.   Thou hast heard an insult, it is the wind; thou art angry, it is a wave. When therefore the wind blows, and the wave swells, the ship is endangered, the heart is in jeopardy, the heart is tossed to and fro. When thou hast heard an insult, thou longest to be avenged; and, lo, avenged thou hast been, and so rejoicing in another's harm thou hast suffered shipwreck. And why is this? Because Christ is asleep in thee. What does this mean, Christ is asleep in thee? Thou hast forgotten Christ. Rouse Him up then, call Christ to mind, let Christ awake in thee, give heed to Him. What didst thou wish? To be avenged. Hast thou forgotten, that when He was being crucified, He said, *Father, forgive them, for they know not what they do?* (Luke 23:34) He who was asleep in thy heart did not wish to be avenged. Awake Him up then, call Him to remembrance. The remembrance of Him is His word; the remembrance of Him is His command. And then wilt thou say if Christ, awake in thee, What manner of man am I, who wish to be avenged! Who am I, who deal out threatenings against another man? I may die perhaps before I am avenged. And when at my last breath, inflamed with rage, and thirsting for vengeance, I shall depart out of this body, He will not receive me, who did not wish to be avenged; He will not receive me, who said, *Give, and it shall be given unto you; forgive, and it shall be forgiven you.* (Luke 6:37-38) Therefore will I refrain myself from my wrath, and return to the repose of my heart. Christ hath commanded the sea, tranquillity is restored.

Sermon 13, 2;
trans. Nicene, 6, 304-305.

197. Meanwhile the ship which carries the disciples, that is, the Church, is tossed and shaken by the tempests of temptation; and the contrary wind, that is, the devil her adversary, rests not, and strives to hinder her from arriving at rest. But greater is *He who maketh intercession for us.* For in this our tossing to and fro in which we toil, He giveth us confidence in coming to us, and strengthening us; only let us not in our trouble throw ourselves out of the ship, and cast ourselves into the sea. For though the ship be in trouble, still it *is* the ship. She alone carrieth the disciples, and receiveth Christ. There is danger, it is true, in the sea; but without her there is instant perishing. Keep thyself therefore in the ship, and pray to God. For when all counsels fail, when even the rudder is unserviceable, and the very spreading of the sails is rather dangerous than useful, when all human help and strength is gone, there remains only for the sailors the earnest cry of entreaty, and pouring out of prayer to God. He then who grants to sailors to reach the haven, shall He so forsake His own Church, as not to bring it on to rest?

Sermon 25, 4;
trans. Nicene, 6, 337-338.

198. As he who sees letters in an excellently written manuscript, and knows not how to read, praises indeed the transcriber's hand, and admires the beauty of the characters; but what those characters mean or signify he does not know; and by the sight of his eyes he is a praiser of the work, but in his mind has no comprehension of it; whereas another man both praises the work, and is capable of understanding it; such a one, I mean, who is not only able to see what is common to all, but who can read also; which he who has never learned cannot. So they who saw Christ's miracles, and understood not what they meant, and what they in a manner conveyed to those who had understanding, wondered only at the miracles themselves; whereas others both wondered at the miracles, and attained to the meaning of them. Such ought we to be in the school of Christ.

Sermon 48, 3;
trans. Nicene, 6, 413.

199. Examine thoroughly man's estate, convict me if I lie: consider all men whether they are in this world for any other end than to be born, to labour, and to die? This is the merchandise of our country: these things here abound. To such merchandise did that Merchantman descend. And forasmuch as every merchant gives and receives; gives what he has, and receives what he has not; when he procures anything, he gives money, and receives what he buys: so Christ too in this His traffic gave and received. But what received He? That which aboundeth here, to be born, to labour, and to die. And what did He give? To be born again, to rise again, and to reign for ever. O Good Merchant, buy us. Why should I say buy us, when we ought to give Thee thanks that Thou hast bought us? Thou dost deal out our Price to us, we drink Thy blood; so dost thou deal out to us our Price. And we read the Gospel, our title deed.

Sermon 80, 2;
trans. Nicene, 6, 499.

200. Why are you sad? Your heart is disturbed by the misfortune in the world, as happened on board the ship in which Christ was sleeping. Notice the reason why your heart is disturbed. The ship in which Christ was sleeping is the heart in which faith is sleeping. Is there anything new in my remarks to you, Christian? In this Christian age the world is being destroyed. Didn't Christ say, the world will be destroyed? Why are you peaceful when the destruction of the world is foretold and disturbed when it is carried out? There is a gale blowing in your heart. Be careful to avoid shipwreck and awaken Christ asleep. The Apostle writes of *Christ dwelling through* *faith in your hearts.* (Eph. 3:17) Christ lives in you by faith. When faith is there, Christ is there. When faith is awake, Christ is awake. But when faith is asleep, Christ is sleeping. Awaken Him saying, *Lord, we are perishing.* (Matt. 8:25)

Sermon 81;
trans. Brady.

201.   *No man cometh unto Me, except the Father which hath sent Me draw him.* (Jo. 6:44) He did not say *lead*, but *draw*. This violence is done to the heart, not the body. Why then dost thou marvel? Believe, and thou comest; love, and thou art drawn. Do not suppose here any rough and uneasy violence; it is gentle, it is sweet; it is the very sweetness that draweth thee. Is not a sheep drawn, when fresh grass is shown to it in its hunger? Yet I imagine that it is not bodily driven on, but fast bound by desire. In such wise do thou come too to Christ; do not conceive of long journeyings; where thou believest, there thou comest. For unto Him, who is everywhere we come by love, not by sailing. But forasmuch as even in this kind of voyage, waves and tempests of divers temptations abound; believe on the Crucified; that thy faith may be able to ascend the Wood. Thou shalt not sink, but shalt be borne upon the Wood. Thus, even thus, amid the waves of this world did he sail, who said, *But God forbid that I should glory, save in the Cross of our Lord Jesus Christ.* (Gal. 6:14)

Sermon 81, 2;
trans. Nicene, 6, 501.

202. Are you seeking happiness? Go to Him who says, *I will give you rest.* (Matt. 11:28) It is in order that you may be taught by Him that He says: *Learn from me, for I am meek and humble of heart.* (*ibid.* 29) You observe your neighbor rich, successful, and proud. By acting as he does, you also will be proud. You will have humility only if you fasten your gaze on Him who became humble for your sake. Christ can teach you what man cannot. He is the correct norm of humility. Whoever comes close to Christ is fashioned according to His humility, that he may later be exalted.

Sermon 126;
trans. Brady.

203. Every human being desires to know the truth and to live. What is the road to these treasures? The philosophers have pointed out erroneous routes. Some have taught one path and others have taught another. The correct way was concealed from them, because *God resists the proud.* (Jas. 4:6) If the true way had not been taught to us, it would also be concealed from us. You asked where is the road: *I am the way.* You asked where is the route: *I am the truth and the life.* (ibid.) You will not stray from the right path if you travel through Him and to Him. This is what Christians teach. Their teaching is more excellent than what philosophers teach, whether it be compared with the sensuality of the Epicureans or with the pride of the Stoics.

Sermon 150;
trans. Brady.

204. *And they who belong to Christ have crucified their flesh with its passions and desires.* (Gal. 5:24) In fact, the Christian ought to be suspended constantly on this cross through his entire life, passed as it is in the midst of temptation. For there is no time in this life when we can tear out the nails of which the Psalmist speaks in the words: *Pierce thou my flesh with thy fear.* (Ps. 118:120) Bodily desires constitute the flesh, and the precepts of justice, the nails with which the fear of the Lord pierces our flesh and crucifies us as victims acceptable to the Lord. Whence the same Apostle says: *I exhort you therefore, brethren, by the mercy of God, to present your bodies as a sacrifice, living, holy, pleasing to God.* (Rom. 12:1)

Hence, there is a cross in regard to which the servant of God, far from being confounded, rejoices, saying: *But as for me, God forbid that I should glory save in the cross of our Lord Jesus Christ, through whom the world is crucified to me, and I to the world.* (Gal. 6:14)

Sermon 205;
trans. FOC 17, 83-84.

205. If you should have a case to be tried before a judge and should procure an advocate, you would be accepted by the lawyer and he would plead your case to the best of his ability. If, before he has finished his plea, you should hear that he is to be the judge, how you would rejoice because he could be your judge who shortly before was your lawyer! Now, the Lord Himself prays for us; He Himself intercedes for us. We have Him as Advocate; would we fear Him as Judge? Nay, rather, because we have sent Him ahead as our Advocate, let us hope that He will be our Judge.

Sermon 213, 5;
trans. FOC 17, 125.

206. Do you wish to be happy? If you wish, I shall show you how you may be happy. Continue to read that passage: *How long will you be dull of heart? why do you love vanity and seek after lying? Know ye—.* What? *that the Lord hath made his holy one wonderful.* (Ps. 4:3-5) Christ came to our miseries. He was hungry and thirsty; He was weary and He slept; He worked wonders and He suffered evils; He was scourged, crowned with thorns, covered with spittle, beaten with cudgels, fixed to a cross, wounded with a lance, placed in a tomb. But He rose again on the third day when His work was finished and death was dead. Lo, keep your eye fixed on His Resurrection, because *the Lord hath made his holy one wonderful* to such a degree that He raised Him from the dead, and bestowed upon Him the honor of sitting at His right hand in heaven. He showed you what you ought to attend to, if you wish to be happy, for here on earth you cannot be happy. In this life you cannot be happy; no one can. You seek what is good, but earth is not the source of that which you seek. What are you seeking? A happy life. But it is not available here. If you were looking for gold in a place where it did not exist, would not he who knew that it was not there say to you: *Why are you digging? Why are you plowing up the earth? You are digging a trench to descend into a place where you will find nothing.* What are you going to answer the one who proffers you this advice? *I am looking for gold.* And he answers: *I do not tell you that what you seek is of no importance, but I do say that it is not in the place where you are looking for it.* Likewise, when you say: *I desire to be happy,* (the answer may be given:) *You seek what is good, but it is not in this place.* If Christ had happiness here, so also will you. But notice what He found in this land of your death. When He came from another region, what did He find here except what abounds here? With you He ate what is plentiful in the cellar of your wretchedness. He drank vinegar here; He had gall, too. Behold, what He found in your cellar!

However, He has invited you to His own table abounding in all good things, the table of heaven, the table of the angels where He Himself is the bread. Coming, then, and finding these unpalatable viands in your cellar, He did not disdain such a table as yours, but He promised you His own.

Sermon 231, 5;
trans. FOC 17, 207-209.

207. In the same way, one who puts on a garment is not changed into that garment, but within it he remains himself, an unchanged man. So, too, if a senator puts on clothing of a slave when, perchance, clothed in his senatorial robes, he cannot enter a prison to console someone who is detained there—if he puts on prison garb, he seems to be wretchedly clothed as far as his physical being is concerned, but interiorly his senatorial dignity remains unimpaired to just such a degree as the mercy was greater by which he was prompted to put on what was of lowly nature. Thus, too, did the Lord, remaining God, remaining the Word, remaining Wisdom, remaining Divine Power, remaining supreme in the administration of the world, yet filling the angels, whole and entire everywhere, in the world, in the patriarchs, in the Prophets, in all the saints, in the womb of the Virgin, (demean Himself) in order to assume human nature, to unite it to Himself as a spouse so that as a Bridegroom He might come forth from the bridechamber and so that He might espouse the Church, a chaste virgin. In this respect, therefore, He was less than the Father because He was man; but equal to the Father because He was God.

Sermon 264, 4; trans. FOC 17, 402-403.

208. Love Christ and seek His light. If a blind person seeks bodily light, how much more ought we to seek the inner light? Let us talk to Him, not with spoken words, but with virtuous deeds. Let us act virtuously, turn away from the world and account everything passing as nothing. If we act in this way, we shall be scolded by those who act from human love, from earthly love, receiving nothing from heaven, taking in deep breaths of fresh air. When they notice us detesting mortal and earthly things, they will surely reprehend us saying, *Why do you put up with this? Why do you act like fools?*

Sermon 349;
trans. Brady.

209. Hence, the word which sounds without is a sign of the word that shines within, to which the name of word more properly belongs. For that which is produced by the mouth of the flesh is the sound of the word, and is itself also called the word, because that inner word assumed it in order that it might appear outwardly. For just as our word in some way becomes a bodily sound by assuming that in which it may be manifested to the senses of men, so the Word of God was made flesh by assuming that in which He might also be manifested to the senses of men. And just as our word becomes a sound and is not changed into a sound, so the Word of God indeed becomes flesh, but far be it from us that it should be changed into flesh. For by assuming it, not by being consumed in it, this word of ours becomes a sound, and that Word became flesh.

On the Trinity, XV, 11,20;
trans. FOC 18, 476-477.

XXV. TRUE CHRISTIAN

210. *Behold, what manner of love the Father hath given unto us, that we should be called, and be, the sons of God.* To be called and not to be, to have the name and not the reality, avails no one. There are many called physicians who cannot cure: there are many called watchers that sleep all night. So are there many called Christians that are not found such in fact; because what they are called they are not in life, in manners, in faith, in hope, in charity.

Epistle of John to the Parthians, IV, 4; trans. Burnaby, 288.

211. For in the kingdom of heaven there are not only those who, that they may be perfect, sell or leave all they have and follow the Lord; but others in the partnership of charity are joined like a mercenary force to the Christian army, to whom it will be said at last, *I was hungry, and ye gave me meat,* and so on. Otherwise, there would be no salvation for those to whom the apostle gives so many anxious and particular directions about their families, telling the wives to be obedient to their husbands, and husbands to love their wives; children to obey their parents, and parents to bring up their children in the instruction and admonition of the Lord; servants to obey with fear their masters according to the flesh, and masters to render to their servants what is just and equal. The apostle is far from condemning such people as regardless of gospel precepts, or unworthy of eternal life.

Against Faustus the Manichee, V, 9;
trans. Nicene, 4, 166.

XXVI. CHURCH

212. For all things that you now see happening in the Church of God, and in the name of Christ throughout the whole world, were already foretold ages before. And even as we read them, so also do we see them; and thereby are we edified unto faith. Once a flood took place over the whole earth, that sinners might be destroyed. And yet those who escaped in the Ark were a figure of the Church that was to be, which now floats upon the waves of the world, and is saved from sinking by the wood of the Cross of Christ.

On Catechizing the Uninstructed, 27, 53; trans. ACW 2, 84.

213. But, just as by means of tokens or marks which we do see we believe the good will of our friends which we do not see, so the Church, which is now visible, is a token of all those past things and a harbinger of future things which are invisible to us, but which are pointed out in the very writings in which she herself is foretold.

Faith in Things Unseen, 5, 8; trans. FOC 2, 464.

214. Even if no testimonies concerning Christ and the Church had appeared in advance, ought not the unexpected illumination of the human race by divine brightness move every one to believe, when we behold false gods abandoned; their images everywhere dashed to pieces; their temples razed or converted to other uses; so many vain rites rooted out from the most inveterate human traditions; and the one true God called upon by all classes of people? And this was brought about by one Man, who was derided by men, seized, bound, scourged, struck, condemned, crucified, and put to death. For His disciples he chose men who were ignorant, inexperienced—fishermen and publicans—through whom His authority should be preserved; men whom He chose as witnesses of His Resurrection and Ascension. And this they have declared that they saw for themselves, and, filled with the Holy Spirit, they have proclaimed the Gospel in all tongues, even those they had never learned. Of those who heard them, some believed; some, not believing, violently withstood their preaching.

Accordingly, the faithful have been struggling, even to the death, for the sake of the truth, not by returning evil for evil, but by bearing evil patiently; they have been victors, not by killing, but by dying. In such a way, then, has the world been changed to this religion; thus have the hearts of all been converted, men and women, young and old, learned and ignorant, wise and simple, mighty and weak, rich and poor, renowned and lowly. And this Church, spread throughout all nations, has so flourished that even now no sect contrary to the Catholic faith, no kind of error, arises which is so much in opposition to the Christian faith that it does not affect and strive to boast in the name of Christ. Indeed, such error would not be permitted to sweep over the earth, were it not for the fact that the very contradiction fosters sound discipline.

Faith in Things Unseen, 7, 10;
trans. FOC 2, 467-468.

XXVII. SACRAMENTS

215. But the baptism of Christ, consecrated by the words of the gospel, is necessarily holy, however polluted and unclean its ministers may be; because its inherent sanctity cannot be polluted, and the divine excellence abides in its sacrament, whether to the salvation of those who use it aright, or to the destruction of those who use it wrong. Would you maintain that, while the light of the sun or of a candle, diffused through unclean places, contracts no foulness in itself therefrom, yet the baptism of Christ can be defiled by the sins of any man, whatsoever he may be? For if we turn our thoughts to the visible materials themselves, which are to us the medium of the sacraments, every one must know that they admit of corruption. But if we think on that which they convey to us, who can fail to see that it is incorruptible, however much the men through whose ministry it is conveyed are either being rewarded or punished for the character of their lives?

On Baptism, Against the Donatists, III, 10; trans. Nicene, 4, 439-440.

216. And in reply to all objections whatsoever, whether we have already answered them separately, or whether they are contained in the remarks of Faustus which we are now considering, we appeal to our established principles, on which we maintain the authority of sacred Scripture. The principle is this, that all things written in the books of the Old Testament are to be received with approval and admiration, as most true and most profitable to eternal life; and that those precepts which are no longer observed outwardly are to be understood as having been most suitable in those times, and are to be viewed as having been shadows of things to come, of which we may now perceive the fulfillments. Accordingly, whoever in those times neglected the observance of these symbolical precepts was righteously condemned to suffer the punishment required by the divine statute, as any one would be now if he were impiously to profane the sacraments of the New Testament, which differ from the old observances only as this time differs from that. For as praise is due to the righteous men of old who refused not to die for the Old Testament sacraments, so it is due to the martyrs of the New Testament. And as a sick man should not find fault with the medical treatment, because one thing is prescribed to-day and another to-morrow, and what was at first required is afterwards forbidden, since the method of cure depends on this; so the human race, sick and sore as it is from Adam to the end of the world, as long as the corrupted body weighs down the mind, (Wisd. 9:15) should not find fault with the divine prescriptions, if sometimes the same observances are enjoined, and sometimes an old observance is exchanged for one of a different kind; especially as there was a promise of a change in the appointments.

Against Faustus the Manichee, XXXII, 14; trans. Nicene, 4, 337.

217. But the Lord, teaching the way of humility, condescended to make use of the sacraments which He found here in reference to the foretelling of His coming, not in order to assist the operation of His cleansing, but as an example for our piety, that so He might show to us with what reverence we ought to receive those sacraments which bear witness that He is already come, when He did not disdain to make use of those which foreshadowed His coming in the future.

Against the Writings of Petilian the Donatist, II, 37.87; trans. Nicene, 4, 553.

XXVIII. MASS

218. There are some who think that, though these visible sacrifices may be suitable for other gods, for the God who is invisible, greater and better, only invisible, greater and better sacrifices, such as the offering of a pure mind and upright will, are appropriate. Such people are evidently ignorant of the fact that these visible sacrifices are mere symbols of invisible sacrifice just as truly as audible words are mere signs of realities. For example, when we direct our prayers and praise to Him, we use words which have meaning and, at the same time, we offer in our hearts the things that our words signify. So, too, when we offer sacrifice, we know that visible sacrifice should be offered to no one but Him to whom we ourselves, in our hearts, should be the invisible sacrifice.

City of God, X, 19;
trans. FOC 7, 151-152.

219. The sacrifice which God had commanded was fitting in those early times, but now it is not so. Therefore, He prescribed another one, fitting for this age, since He knew much better than man what is suitably adapted to each age, and, being the unchangeable Creator as well as Ruler of the world of change, He knows as well what and when to give, to add to, to take away, to withdraw, to increase, or to diminish, until the beauty of the entire world, of which the individual parts are suitable each for its own time, swells, as it were, into a mighty song of some unutterable musician, and from thence the true adorers of God rise to the eternal contemplation of His face, even in time of faith.

Letter 138, to Marcellinus;
trans. FOC 11, 39.

FOR FURTHER READING...

Mystical Union with God
Through the Nine Degrees of Prayer

Rev. James Alberione, SSP, STD

Drawn from a series of conferences on prayer, this brief volume answers the aspiration of all those who want to elevate their prayer life for a closer union with God. Basing himself mainly on the spirituality of Teresa of Avila, Father Alberione offers a down-to-earth presentation of the nine degrees of prayer, thus opening to everyone the Gospel challenge: "You must be perfect as your heavenly Father is perfect." 76 pages
paper $1.50 — SP0460

Holiness in the Church

Rev. John A. Hardon, SJ

A volume of timely reflections on the spiritual life. For priests, religious and laity: a stimulus to all to become holier. 179 pages
cloth $3.50; paper $2.50 — SP0250

How To Converse Continually and Familiarly with God
St. Alphonsus de Liguori
An excellent translation of a little masterpiece that breathes confidence in God through every line, inculcating the practice of speaking intimately with Him.
80 pages
cloth $2.25 — SP0260

The Imitation of Christ
Thomas à Kempis
440 pages
flexible plastic $3.50 — SP0290
imitation leather $5.25

In Praise of St. Paul
St. John Chrysostom
Translated by Halton, Ph.D. The sermons contained in this volume testify to the saint's knowledge of St. Paul's writings as well as to his deep admiration of Paul's many virtues. 128 pages
cloth $2.00 — SP0300

The Last Things
Rev. James Alberione, SSP, STD

Life will never look the same again when one has finished this book. Behind every event the mind's horizon envisions eternity. "A fine collection of spiritual thoughts and prayers that might well serve as a personal 'do-it-yourself' retreat." "Today's Family." 360 pages
cloth $4.50 — SP0350

For Inner Peace and Strength
Don Costello

Meditative prayers for the ups and downs encountered daily: Courage to stand firm; Friendliness that shares and sacrifices; Patience that knows no season; Prudence for a multitude of choices; Contemplation, a fruitful experience; Truth's vital fibres; Life plus eternity. 140 pages
cloth $4.00; paper $3.00 — SP0169

Order from addresses on the following page. Please specify title and item number.

Daughters of St. Paul

IN MASSACHUSETTS
  50 St. Paul's Ave. Jamaica Plain, Boston, MA 02130;
    617-522-8911; 617-522-0875;
  172 Tremont Street, Boston, MA 02111; **617-426-5464;
    617-426-4230**
IN NEW YORK
  78 Fort Place, Staten Island, NY 10301; **212-447-5071**
  59 East 43rd Street, New York, NY 10017; **212-986-7580**
  7 State Street, New York, NY 10004; **212-447-5071**
  625 East 187th Street, Bronx, NY 10458; **212-584-0440**
  525 Main Street, Buffalo, NY 14203; **716-847-6044**
IN NEW JERSEY
  Hudson Mall — Route 440 and Communipaw Ave.,
    Jersey City, NJ 07304; **201-433-7740**
IN CONNECTICUT
  202 Fairfield Ave., Bridgeport, CT 06604; **203-335-9913**
IN OHIO
  2105 Ontario St. (at Prospect Ave.), Cleveland, OH 44115; **216-621-9427**
  25 E. Eighth Street, Cincinnati, OH 45202; **513-721-4838**
IN PENNSYLVANIA
  1719 Chestnut Street, Philadelphia, PA 19103; **215-568-2638**
IN FLORIDA
  2700 Biscayne Blvd., Miami, FL 33137; **305-573-1618**
IN LOUISIANA
  4403 Veterans Memorial Blvd., Metairie, LA 70002; **504-887-7631;
    504-887-0113**
  1800 South Acadian Thruway, P.O. Box 2028, Baton Rouge, LA 70821
    504-343-4057; 504-343-3814
IN MISSOURI
  1001 Pine Street (at North 10th), St. Louis, MO 63101; **314-621-0346;
    314-231-1034**
IN ILLINOIS
  172 North Michigan Ave., Chicago, IL 60601; **312-346-4228**
IN TEXAS
  114 Main Plaza, San Antonio, TX 78205; **512-224-8101**
IN CALIFORNIA
  1570 Fifth Avenue, San Diego, CA 92101; **714-232-1442**
  46 Geary Street, San Francisco, CA 94108; **415-781-5180**
IN HAWAII
  1143 Bishop Street, Honolulu, HI 96813; **808-521-2731**
IN ALASKA
  750 West 5th Avenue, Anchorage AK 99501; **907-272-8183**
IN CANADA
  3022 Dufferin Street, Toronto 395, Ontario, Canada
IN ENGLAND
  128, Notting Hill Gate, London W11 3QG, England
  133 Corporation Street, Birmingham B4 6PH, England
  5A-7 Royal Exchange Square, Glasgow G1 3AH, England
  82 Bold Street, Liverpool L1 4HR, England
IN AUSTRALIA
  58 Abbotsford Rd., Homebush, N.S.W., Sydney 2140, Australia